Ultimate
NECKLACE MAKER

D&C
David and Charles
www.mycraftivity.com

A DAVID & CHARLES BOOK
Copyright © David & Charles Limited 2009

David & Charles is an F+W Media Inc. company
4700 East Galbraith Road
Cincinnati, OH 45236

First published in the UK in 2009

Text and designs copyright © Dorothy Wood 2009
Photography and illustrations copyright © David & Charles 2009

A catalogue record for this book is available from the British Library.

ISBN-13: 978-0-7153-3169-9 paperback
ISBN-10: 0-7153-3169-8 paperback

Printed in China by R R Donnelley
for David & Charles
Brunel House   Newton Abbot   Devon

Senior Commissioning Editor: Cheryl Brown
Editor: Bethany Dymond
Assistant Editor: Kate Nicholson
Project Editor: Jo Richardson
Art Editor: Charly Bailey
Designer: Mia Farrant
Art Direction: Sarah Underhill
Production Controller: Bev Richardson
Photography: Lorna Yabsley, Ally Stuart, Kim Sayer, Karl Adamson and Simon Whitmore
Illustration: Ethan Danielson and Mia Farrant

Visit our website at www.davidandcharles.co.uk

David & Charles books are available from all good bookshops; alternatively you can contact
our Orderline on 0870 9908222 or write to us at FREEPOST EX2 110, D&C Direct, Newton
Abbot, TQ12 4ZZ (no stamp required UK only); US customers call 800-289-0963 and Canadian
customers call 800-840-5220.

To Cheryl – it's been a pleasure.

Contents

Introduction

How many times have you gone up to someone and said, 'I love your necklace'? I've certainly done so dozens of times. Necklaces seem naturally to attract that sort of attention, perhaps initially as they are at eye level, but also because they have usually been carefully chosen to match the style and colour of what the person is wearing. I often add, 'Where did you get it?', although if I'm at a bead fair or craft show I'm more likely to ask, 'Did you make it yourself?' My response is then one of sheer delight if the necklace turns out to be handmade.

Necklace colours, shapes and lengths are always evolving as fashions change from season to season, but over the years the same styles reappear time and time again. In this book I have identified the ten fundamental necklace styles, namely single-strand, pendant, multi-strand, bib, Y-shaped, collar, lariat, sautoir, knotted and floating. Each chapter focuses in turn on one of these great classic styles, revealing the essential characteristics of its design. I then explore how each necklace style can be re-imagined to suit every taste and occasion.

For example, a cool and chic single strand of pearls and large white turquoise beads is contrastingly reinterpreted as a wild mosaic design of red and gold elements, while a formal collar of glowing orange and rich reds with an ornate clasp is reincarnated Egyptian-style in a ribbon-tied band of exotic silver basket and turquoise beads. The super-long sautoir first appears as an arty iridescent bead-stitched rope and beaded tassel and later as a vintage design of antique gold chains interspersed with chunky bronze beads.

Instructions for making 15 of these necklace designs are presented in step-by-step detail, and encompass a wide variety of techniques, from stringing and knotting to wirework and bead stitching. The opening section of the book also offers a guide to the main types of bead and bead finishes, how to select and combine colours, what stringing materials, findings and fastenings to use and the

tools and equipment you will need, together with advice on designing your own necklaces. At the back of the book you will find a comprehensive and practical resource covering all the jewellery techniques involved in making the projects, including working with cord and threads, wire and chain, using headpins and other findings, adding fastenings, spacing beads and working bead stitches and knots.

With over 40 handmade necklace designs on offer, along with a range of complementary jewellery projects, such as rings, bracelets, brooches and earrings, you will simply be spoilt for choice. That little phrase, 'I love your necklace' was the inspiration for this book, and I'm sure when someone asks, you will be proud to say, 'I made it myself'.

Bead Basics

The necklaces in this book are made from a wide variety of beads, but these represent only a tiny proportion of the wealth available. There are innumerable colours, textures, shapes and sizes of bead to suit every style of necklace, and much of the enjoyment in making your own jewellery comes from searching for the ideal beads. The following advice will help you make the appropriate choices to achieve the best results and to maximize your bead shopping pleasure, including a guide to the most popular bead types, how they are measured and the different finishes available, as well as how to compose with colour.

Shopping for beads

Many bead shops specialize in particular types of bead, such as large decorative beads or, by contrast, smaller beads such as seed beads and bugles, and the range on offer will also frequently reflect the individual taste and style of the buyer or owner. It is a real bonus to find the perfect shop in your own locality, but if you don't have ready access to a bead shop or can't find the beads you require, the internet makes it easy to buy beads from around the world, delivered to your door in a few days. Although postage is an additional cost, it is often still a more economical way to purchase them.

With such an overwhelming variety of beads available, it can be difficult deciding what to buy. If you are new to beading or jewellery making, choose the same or similar beads that were actually used in the projects (see Bead Details, pages 125–126), then once you are feeling more confident, have fun selecting your own for a unique design.

Beads Decoded - Bead finish guide

The availability of such a huge variety of beads, especially those made from glass, stems from the wide range of finishes on offer. When buying seed beads and bugles in particular, several terms are often used to explain exactly what the bead looks like, and becoming familiar with these will also help you choose larger glass beads. For example, 'SL purple AB' is a silver-lined purple bead with an iridescent, rainbow effect on the surface ('AB' meaning 'aurora borealis'). Such descriptive detail can be extremely useful when you are ordering from a catalogue or on the internet where there are lots of different types of similar-looking and coloured beads.

⊙ **Transparent** beads made from clear or coloured glass are see-through, allowing the passage of light.

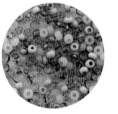

⊙ **Opaque** beads have a solid colour that doesn't allow any light to pass through.

⊙ **Translucent** beads are between transparent and opaque and are sometimes known as **greasy**, **opal** or **satin** beads.

⊙ **Gloss** beads are very shiny like glass.

⊙ **Matt** beads are opaque beads that have been tumbled or dipped in acid to give them a dull, flat surface.

⊙ **Frosted** beads are transparent or translucent beads that have been treated in a similar way to matt beads.

⊙ **Dyed** beads have been painted with a dye or paint on the surface. They often have bright or unusual colours, but the dye or paint can wear off in use.

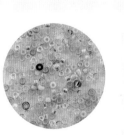

⊙ **Colour-lined** or **inside colour** beads are transparent with the hole lined in another opaque colour.

⊙ **Silver-lined** (**rocaille**) beads have the hole lined with silver and look really sparkly. Sometimes the hole is square to enhance the shine. They are also available with a matt finish that has a frosted appearance.

⊙ **Iris, iridescent, rainbow** or **AB** beads have been treated with metal salts while the glass is hot to create a coating that resembles an oil slick. On matt beads, this can produce an appearance like raku or pottery-fired clay.

⊙ **Lustre** beads are opaque beads with a coating that gives the bead a pearl finish.

⊙ **Ceylon** beads are transparent with a milky lustre.

⊙ **Gold** or **silver lustre** beads have been treated with a gold or silver pearl finish.

⊙ **Metallic** beads have been heated and sprayed with oxidized tin.

⊙ **Higher metallic** beads are surface-coated with gold and then sprayed with oxidized titanium, the gold creating a brighter finish.

⊙ **Galvanized** beads are electroplated with zinc and have a more durable finish.

Large and lustrous

Glass beads

The most versatile of all the bead materials, glass can be made into all kinds of sizes and shapes, ranging in quality from transparent to opaque, and with a variety of finishes (see page 7). **Pressed glass** beads are made in moulds to form lots of different shapes, from leaves and flowers to discs, cylinders and drops, while cracked glass beads look like cubes or pieces of ice that have shattered with the change in temperature. High-quality faceted **Czech firepolish** beads, available in a wide range of sizes and shapes, are ideal for necklaces – see the sumptuous Hot Property collar on pages 66–71 – and look fabulous with an AB finish (see page 7). **Millefiori** beads are made from canes of glass in the same way as seaside rock and then cut into slices to reveal the decorative cross section. Hollow and extremely lightweight, **blown glass** beads are available in stunning patterns and colours, and look particularly attractive in a heart-shaped pendant bead.

Lampwork beads

These exquisite glass beads, featured in the Lovely Lampwork single-strand necklace on page 33, are handmade with rods or canes of plain or patterned glass using a blowtorch, so although you can replicate the production process, no two beads are ever identical. Lampwork as a craft has boomed in recent years and consequently there are many contemporary styles to choose from. The base bead, formed around a revolving metal rod or mandrel that determines the size of the hole, can be decorated with more glass and shaped using a variety of techniques. Top-quality Venetian lampwork beads from Murano often have metal foil linings that sparkle through the transparent glass.

Crystals

The term 'crystal' describes a faceted bead ranging from the finest-quality cut glass, such as Swarovski crystals, to inexpensive faceted glass or even moulded plastic beads. There is a huge variation in price, but as always, you get what you pay for and the more expensive crystals like Swarovski have a far superior shine and sparkle. Firepolish beads are high-quality but reasonably priced beads available in larger sizes, and are ideal for chunky necklaces. The Crystal Falls floating necklace on page 110 features a combination of Swarovski crystals and firepolish beads in fabulous shades of pink and purple.

Pearls

It is easy to distinguish between real and fake pearls: if you rub a real pearl gently against your tooth it produces a grating sensation, whereas the surface of imitation pearls is completely smooth. Real pearls, which fall into the organic group (see opposite), can either be cultured (from a pearl farm) or from the wild. Like every other type of bead the price varies with quality; the most valuable pearls have an iridescent lustre and are not overly wrinkled. In the Pearly Queen 'Y'-shaped necklace on pages 58–63, subtle shades of pearl are set off by fine silver filigree caps. Glass pearl beads have the gorgeous lustre applied to a glass bead. Available in a range of fashion colours, rather than the usual white, cream or pastel shades, they can be quite large, making them ideal for contemporary necklaces.

Metal beads

These come in a wide range of materials, such as brass, copper, aluminium and different alloys. Some silver and gold beads are plated over a base metal, but you can buy precious metal beads in sterling silver. As gold is so expensive, beads are generally made from a cheaper substitute known as rolled or gold-filled. Metal beads often have a distinctive textured surface and can be moulded, modelled or shaped from sheet metal. These hollow metal beads are surprisingly light and useful for longer necklace styles like lariats and sautoirs, such as the bronze examples used in the Linked in Time sautoir on page 90.

Modelled beads

Materials for modelling beads include resin, gesso, lacquer, papier mâché, ceramic, polymer clay and cinnabar. Although many are mass-produced, these beads are still in the main handmade and have a quaintness and individuality that can't be found in manufactured beads. See the Rustic Charm lariat design on page 83.

Plastic beads

These range from the cheap and cheerful to highly collectable early plastics beads like bakelite and vulcanite. More recent plastics include perspex, acetate and coloured cast resins. Plastic beads can be dyed or coated – the citrus-coloured examples in Funky Lime on pages 108–109 show just how distinctive they can be. Metallic coatings look surprisingly authentic; they are lighter than metal beads and ideal for longer necklaces.

Gemstones or semi-precious beads

These are pieces of mineral that have been cut and polished to make extremely attractive and valuable beads, such as the volcanic-looking black agate and glossy black onyx beads, both forms of quartz, in the Midnight and Moonshine sautoir on page 91. Some rocks such as lapis lazuli and organic materials like amber or jet are also considered to be gemstones. Often sold in strings, the price varies considerably depending on the aesthetic value and rarity of the mineral. Transparent gemstones are sometimes faceted to add sparkle and opaque gemstones like opal are often made into cabochons. Some semi-precious stones, such as jade, are dyed to produce a more varied range of colours. Inexpensive chips are small, rough pieces of mineral that look stunning when crocheted with wire.

Organic

Fashioned from seeds, nuts, shells, bones and horn, these were the first beads made by our ancestors for artistic ornamentation and are still popular today. Some organic materials like ivory, amber, tortoiseshell and jet are now rare, but can be found in antique jewellery. Painted wood beads are colourful and cheap, such as those used in the Wood Works knotted necklace on page 100, and there are also many attractive beads available made from unusual woods from around the world.

Small and stylish

Seed beads

These are round, donut-shaped beads ranging from size 3 to size 15. Combinations of different shades and sizes can look especially effective, as in the 1930s-inspired Lilac Loops collar design on pages 72–73. Larger seed beads are known as **pebble beads** and the smaller ones as **petites**.

Cylinder beads

Also known by their trade names **Delicas**, **Antiques** or **Magnificas**, these precision-milled tubular beads have a large hole, enabling you to pass the thread through each bead several times. They are ideal for bead stitching because of their uniform size. Cylinder beads are available in the same range of colours and finishes as seed beads (see left). Look out for **double Delicas**, which are much larger and available smooth or with a hex finish. The large hole in double Delicas allows the beads to be threaded on to thicker threads such as fine waxed cord. The Twist and Snake bead-stitched lariat on pages 76–80 combines double Delicas with seed beads and short bugles to make an attractively textured rope.

Hex beads

These are cylindrical beads made from a six-sided glass cane, and are like a squat bugle (see opposite). They are useful for creating texture. **Twisted hex beads**, also called two-cuts, can be silver-lined, adding extra sparkle to necklaces such as the Silver Sensation floating necklace on pages 102–107.

Papillon beads

These are a new style of rocaille seed bead that have a distinctive shape. The beads look a little like butterfly wings, hence the name, and because of the irregular shape and the way the beads sit haphazardly when strung, they can add a wonderful texture to necklace designs, such as Shimmering Swirl on page 48.

Triangle beads

As their name indicates, these have three sides and add an interesting texture to beaded fabric, especially herringbone stitch. There are two main styles both from Japan: the geometric sharp-sided **Toho triangle**, used in the Horn of Plenty multi-strand necklace on pages 42–47, and the more rounded **Miyuki triangle**, used in Pebble Dangles on pages 30–31. Miyuki triangles look particularly attractive if they are silver-lined to add extra sparkle, and look out for the stunning matt metallic Toho triangles with an iris finish.

Bugle beads

These are glass canes cut to a variety of lengths. The most common sizes are 3–4mm, 6–7mm, 9mm and 15mm. Bugle beads can be matched to seed beads (see opposite): the smallest bugles are the same size as size 12 seed beads and the other bugles match size 11 seed beads. **Twisted bugles** are five- or six-sided tubes that have been twisted while the glass is still hot. The herringbone-stitched Peacock Plume sautoir on pages 84–88 is quick to work using long twisted bugles, and also includes short bugles, seed beads and Toho triangles (see left).

Beads Decoded – Bead size guide

It is useful to know how the common bead shapes are measured, especially when buying from a catalogue or online, as they are not always illustrated actual size.

⊙ **Large** beads are measured in millimetres.

⊙ **Round** beads are measured by the diameter.

⊙ **Long** beads, such as ovals, droplets and cylinders, are measured by length and width.

⊙ **Cubes and bicone** beads, which look like two pyramids stuck together, are measured across the width.

⊙ **Seed beads or rocailles**, traditionally sold by size or aughts

(expressed as 11/0 or 110) are now commonly sold by diameter measurement. Although makes vary, 1.8mm diameter seed beads should be equivalent to 11/0, 2.2mm to 9/0 and 3.3mm to 6/0. Seed beads range from tiny petite beads (size 15 or 1.3mm) to larger pebble beads (size 3 or 5.5mm), but the most popular sizes are size 9, size 10 (2mm) or size 11.

⊙ **Bugle** beads, which are thin glass tubes, can be sold by length in millimetres or by size, and Czech and Japanese bugles are measured differently. If matching bugles with seed beads in diameter, size 1 bugles are about the same diameter as a size 12 seed bead (1.9mm); other bugles are about the same diameter as a size 11 (1.8mm) seed bead.

Creating with colour

Choosing and combining different colours of bead to create an attractive necklace can be daunting. Many of us feel that we don't know a great deal about what colours work together, but we do, in fact, make good colour choices all the time without thinking. Look around your home, in the garden or in your wardrobe and you will find plenty of colour schemes that you have devised yourself.

Harmonizing colours

People often make the mistake of thinking that harmonious colours are necessarily drawn from the same section of the colour wheel (see right), but harmony simply means a pleasing combination. For instance, the Lime and Raspberry Splash sautoir on page 91 uses two quite different colours, yet they work well together. Next time you are in a bead shop, take a container and choose a few beads in a colour that you like. As you add some beads in different colours and take away others, you will see how the balance of the colours change. Instinctively, you will end up with a mix of beads that will harmonize in a necklace design. If you need extra reassurance, start with a bead you like that has more than one colour and then choose other beads that match the various colours. This is how the beads for the Juicy Mosaic single-strand necklace on page 33 were selected. Adding gold or silver often helps to lift the colours and adds a little zing.

Making a colour palette

Before going bead shopping, draw inspiration from all around you for suitable ideas on colour. Colour combinations found in nature always work well or look for effective colour schemes in the home, such as a favourite garment, a pretty postcard, a funky tablemat or a gorgeous contemporary vase. Paint or cut swatches of these colours from magazines to create a colour palette, but bear in mind that you will only achieve the same overall effect if you get the proportions right. Study how much there is of each colour, for example 50 per cent in a soft green, 25 per cent in lilac, 20 per cent in dark cream and 5 per cent in yellow-green, then select bead quantities in the same colours to match.

Colour know-how

Colour theory is a complex science, but the colour wheel is an easy and practical tool for any bead worker to use. The basic wheel is based on the three primary colours, three secondary colours and six tertiary colours, but the colour range can be extended to 36 colours with tints and shades of each colour.

Use the colour wheel to create the harmonious schemes opposite, although it doesn't tell you the proportion of each colour to use, so experiment and have fun!

Monochromatic colour schemes look clean and elegant, and are very easy on the eyes, especially in blues or greens. Choose one colour and then paler tints and darker shades of the same colour. This colour scheme always looks balanced and visually appealing, but is rarely vibrant.

Split complementary colour schemes use one colour and two colours that sit either side of its complementary colour. This creates a subtler effect than straight complementary colours and works really well if you use a single warm colour and several cool colours or vice versa.

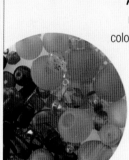

Analogous colour schemes are often referred to as 'cool colours' or 'warm colours', as they use adjacent colours on the colour wheel. They have a richer appearance than monochromatic schemes. Choose one colour as the dominant colour and the other one or two to enrich the scheme.

Triadic colour schemes use three colours equally spaced around the colour wheel. It is a popular scheme because it offers strong contrasts and richness while retaining a balanced effect. Use more of one colour than the others, and if the beads look gaudy, tone the colours down slightly.

Complementary colour schemes use two colours opposite one another on the colour wheel for a strong contrast and work best when you put a cool colour, such as green/blue, against a warm colour, for example red. Choose one of the colours as the main colour and use the other as an accent.

Tetradic colour schemes use two colours and their complementary colours. This is one of the most vibrant schemes, using a great variety of colours, but as a result it can be difficult to balance harmoniously. It works better if you choose one colour to be dominant or tone down the colours.

Bead hole know-how

All beads, unless they are a cabochon, have a hole of some sort to feed a thread, wire or cord through.

Positioning

Most holes are in the centre of the bead, either vertical or horizontal, but some are off-centre, going through the back like a button with a shank or at one end. Drop beads have a hole running vertically through the bead or across the top so that the bead hangs down attractively.

Look closely at the photographs of the finished necklaces to see where the bead holes are positioned before you buy your beads.

Size

The size of the hole varies and is not always in proportion to the size of the bead. Pandora beads (with a sterling silver or silver-plated core), for example, are made to fit over a thick cord or metal chain and have a very large hole (see Chain Reaction, page 83). If you are planning to use a particular thread, bead string or cord, check the hole size of your chosen beads, especially if you are ordering from a catalogue or online.

It can be frustrating when you find the perfect bead for your necklace but some of the holes are not the right size. You can, however, take steps to remedy this, as follows.

Enlarging holes

If the hole is slightly too small or blocked, often an issue with pearls or clay beads, you can use a bead reamer to open out the hole slightly. This has several different file ends to suit different beads (see page 21).

Large-hole solutions

If the bead hole is too large, there are several ways to resolve the problem.

⊙ **Providing support**
The simplest technique is to use a filigree cap (see page 19) so that the bead is supported centrally. If the bead hole is large you can fill with small seed beads first.

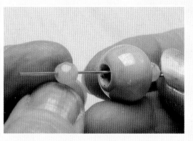

⊙ **Using beads**
Add a bead with smaller holes each side so that the larger bead is supported centrally on the headpin, wire or thread.

⊙ **Filling with polymer clay**
Polymer clay can be used to fill larger holes. Choose or mix a clay colour similar to the bead and use to fill the hole. Push a headpin, or thicker wire for a larger hole, through the centre of the clay, place on a baking tray and bake in a preheated domestic oven at 110°C (225°F) or Gas Mark ¼ for 20 minutes, or according to the manufacturer's instructions. Leave to cool, then remove the headpin or wire. Most ceramic and glass beads can be baked – if in doubt, test first with one bead.

Winning Stringing

There are dozens of traditional threads for bead stringing as well as new stringing materials appearing all the time, so knowing which to choose for your necklace can be quite a predicament. Think about the design of the necklace; whether the threads will be hidden or an integral part of the design; if you are planning a chunky design or something more delicate; and whether you have particular beads in mind. Consider the weight of the beads and use the strongest thread you can, preferably in a double thickness for extra security. Be guided by looking at similar designs in the book or use the following guide to help you choose the perfect stringing material for your design.

Thicker materials

Leather thong

This round, glossy stringing material is ideal for pendants or stringing beads with large holes. Generally available 1–2mm (about ¹⁄₁₆in) thick.

Soft suede

A flat strip that is matt, with the characteristic rough texture of suede. It can be natural, but is more likely to be faux suede. Usually about 2.5 or 3mm thick (about ⅛in).

Waxed cotton

This popular cotton cord is pre-waxed and ideal for knotted necklaces and bracelets. The most common thicknesses are 0.5–2mm (0.02–0.079in).

Satin cord

A soft, silky cord also known as rattail. Mousetail and bugtail are progressively thinner.

Hemp

This traditional macramé cord is once again becoming popular and is ideal for knotted necklaces or for stringing natural beads.

Types of thread

There is a dauntingly vast array of stringing threads available, made from a variety of fibres in a wide range of thicknesses. Fortunately, the style of the necklace, type of beads and method of construction will help to narrow the choice considerably. Each necklace featured in the book has a recommended thread, but you can find out more and make your own choice by using the following guide.

Multifilaments

This thread group is used primarily for bead stitching and is designed to be hidden by the beads. The parallel fibre threads are pre-waxed and lightly twisted. They are tangle-resistant, colourfast and can be tied in a tight knot. Trade names include Nymo, KO, One-G and Superlon. Each has slightly different properties; for example Nymo has a slight stretch and a flat cross section, whereas KO has no stretch and a circular cross section, so do check before choosing.

Monofilaments

These are threads with a single strand and include elastic thread, illusion cord, parachute cord and fishing line. Illusion cord or Supplemax are two makes of this clear beading thread, which is used to make illusion or floating necklaces (see pages 102–111). Elastic threads such as Stretch Magic or Opelon don't require fastenings; the knot can be hidden inside a bead.

Braided threads

These are made from multi-strands that have been plaited (braided) together to make a very strong thread that doesn't stretch. Power Pro, Grandslam and Fireline were all originally makes of fishing line, but are now used extensively for beading. Designed to be hidden between the beads, they are especially good for stringing or stitching beads with sharp edges, such as crystals and bugles. Fireline boasts the highest strength per diameter of threads on the market, while Grandslam is available up to 0.46mm (0.018in), which is ideal for bigger beads.

Bead cords

These unwaxed twisted threads are designed to be visually attractive and used for necklaces where you want the thread to be seen. Traditionally made from silk and used for knotting strings of pearls, the cords are now available in nylon, a stronger but much stiffer thread than silk. Silk threads are relative short-lived and beads may need restringing after three to five years. Silk cord trade names include Gudebrod and Griffin; Strength, Griffin, Conso and C-lon are nylon cords. If you don't want the thread colour to show through clear beads, use C-thru nylon thread.

Twisted threads

Waxed two-ply beading threads have been available for many years and are ideal for bead stringing or bead stitching where the thread is hidden by the beads. Waxed threads are less likely to break than unwaxed thread. One of the most popular types is Silamide size A or O. Kevlar thread is extremely strong, but you need to use a fishermen's knot such as a figure-of-eight (see page 124) to secure.

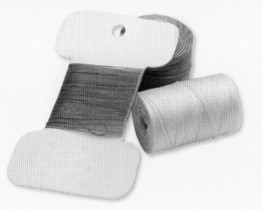

Bead stringing wire

This versatile stringing material is most commonly used for floating necklaces (see pages 102–111), but is actually ideal for any necklace where you want the beads to hang in a smooth, soft curve. It is composed of tiny wires twisted together and coated with nylon thread. The number of tiny wires, also known as strands, determines the flexibility of the wire – the greater the number, the more flexible the wire will be. The 7-strand variety holds its shape better than 19-strand wire but is not as flexible, while 49-strand wire is the most flexible. These nylon-coated wires include Acculon's tigertail, Softflex and Beadalon stringing wire. Some bead stringing wires can be knotted, but usually the wire is secured with crimps (see page 115).

Threads Decoded – Thicknesses

Most threading materials come in a variety of thicknesses, and you will need to match the thickness to the size of your bead holes to avoid loose beads rubbing against the thread, which will create friction and increase the likelihood of the thread snapping. In general, use a double strand of a thinner thread, as it is more secure than a single strand of a thicker thread. Thread sizes vary depending on the make, with either a letter or number indicating the size.

⊙ Letter sizes range from 00, which is the finest, through A, B, C, D, E, F and FF to G, the thickest. D is ideal for bead stitching with seed beads, E or F for medium-weight beads and F or G for heavy beads.

⊙ Weight strengths are given for threads that were originally fishing line, such as Fireline, Grandslam and Power Pro, and range from 4–80lb (0.06–0.46mm). A 4lb line is equivalent to size B and a 6lb line to size D.

Nymo™ B

SuperLon™ D

Silamide size A

Nylon thread size 4

Silk size 5 /0.68mm

Silk size 10 /0.9mm

Wax cotton 0.8mm

Wax cotton 1mm

Rattail

Leather thong

Finishing Touches

To finish off your necklace, you will need a range of metal supporting or linking components, known as findings, as well as an appropriate fastening. Findings and fastenings are available in a range of metallic finishes, as well as the traditional silver and gold. Those made from sterling silver are obviously more expensive, but add an extra dimension of quality to jewellery.

Findings

These utilitarian items have traditionally remained 'behind the scenes' in jewellery, but in recent years, some have become as crucial to contemporary necklace designs as the beads themselves, such as the antique silver spacer bars used to dynamic effect in the Miracle Bars collar on page 74.

Headpins

These resemble a large dressmaker's pin and are used to make bead dangles or charms (see pages 118–119). Basic headpins have a flat, plain end, but look out for headpins with decorative ends, which are especially attractive for making earrings.

Eyepins

These have a round loop at one end and are generally used to make bead links (see pages 118–119). Longer eyepins can be coiled to make decorative ends for earrings or pendants.

Thong ends

Secure to the ends of leather thong or cord using flat-nosed pliers so that a fastening can be attached (see page 114).

Spring ends

Thread ribbons and cords into the springs, then squeeze the end spring only to secure and attach a fastening (see page 114).

Crimp ends

These findings are specially designed for finishing bead stringing wire neatly, but can also be used for fine thong and other threads. Simply insert the wire and squeeze the crimp end with crimping pliers (see Step 3, page 73).

Knot covers

Also known as calottes (with a side hole) or clamshell calottes (with a hole in the hinge), these findings hide the knot or crimp at the end of the necklace and make it easy to attach a fastening (see page 114).

End cones

These are knot covers, usually cone- or tulip-shaped, for thicker threads, ribbons or multiple strands. Choose a size that fits snugly around the beads. See page 115 for how to secure the threads and attach fastenings.

End bars

Use end bars with rings for attaching multiple strands of beads on necklaces and bracelets. Solid bars have tiny teeth for gripping and can be secured to ribbon, yarn or beadwork with flat-nosed pliers.

Spacer bars

These hold strings of beads at an equal distance apart. Use end bars with the same number of rings or holes to finish the necklace, then attach the fastening (see pages 114–115).

Crimps

Round and tubular crimps are generally used on thread that can't be knotted, such as bead stringing wire. They are available in a range of sizes – generally use a larger size of tube than the round style. To attach fastenings and space beads along the wire, see pages 114–116.

Jump rings

These round or oval rings, which have a slit for opening and closing, are generally used to link components and attach fastenings (see pages 114 and 120–121). They can also be used for chain maille where rings are linked together in a decorative pattern, such as in the Bohemian Rhapsody design on pages 50–55.

Split rings

These are formed from a coil of wire. The fastening has to be slotted between the coils and pushed round to secure over both wires. Use split-ring pliers to attach fastenings to prevent breaking your fingernails.

Solid rings

Available in a diverse range of sizes and shapes, solid rings are used generally as a design element in necklace making, either individually or joined together with jump rings to make a chain – see Rings and Things, page 57.

Bead sieves

There are lots of different sieve components to make brooches, scarf clips or rings. The sieves are simply mesh or punched metal that can be decorated by 'sewing' on beads using wire or thread (see page 123).

Filigree caps

These give a slightly antique appearance to beads. There are lots of different styles and sizes to suit a range of beads.

Earring wires

These come in a variety of styles suitable for pierced ears, or you can buy screw or clip fitments. See page 119 for how to attach.

Fastenings

These range from the basic lobster claw to ornate toggle and clasp items. Choose one to suit the style or material used to make the necklace, making sure that it is strong enough for the weight of the beads. Fastenings can have a single hole or multiple holes to accommodate one or more strands. Crimp fastenings are ideal for bead stringing wire or fine thong, as you can slot the threading material straight into the fastening and secure with crimping pliers.

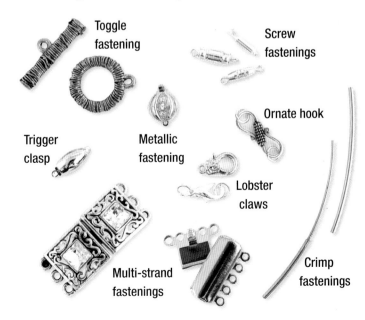

Toggle fastening

Screw fastenings

Ornate hook

Trigger clasp

Metallic fastening

Lobster claws

Multi-strand fastenings

Crimp fastenings

Tools of the Trade

As with any craft, if you are new to jewellery making, you will need to assemble a small range of basic tools (see below). As you progress, you can invest in one or two of the more specialist tools and other equipment as required. Beadwork tools and equipment are readily available from craft and bead shops or from one of the many online suppliers, some of which are listed on page 127.

Basic tool kit

Choose a relatively fine set of these tools, as you will usually be working on a small scale. Mini tools are ideal if you have small hands or intend to make only one or two necklaces in a week.

Flat-nosed pliers

These pliers have flat jaws with a slightly rough surface to grip wire or findings. Some are called snipe- or chain-nosed pliers, which taper towards the tip, and others have a blunt end (blunt-nosed).

Round-nosed pliers

These have tubular tapered jaws and are used for coiling, bending wire and making jump rings. Work near the tip of the jaws for tiny loops, but towards the base for larger rings.

Wire cutters

Also known as flush cutters, this tool has a flat side so that you can cut wire to leave a straight end. For jewellery making, a small pair with fine tips gives better results, as you can work closer in to trim wire ends neatly.

Beading mat

Textured mats are inexpensive and indispensable for all beading work. The fine pile stops the beads rolling about and lets you pick up directly on to the needle. Once you have finished, it is easy to fold the mat and tip any beads left back into their container.

Embroidery scissors

These small scissors with fine, sharp points are ideal for trimming the ends of threads closely, especially in the case of small-scale work.

Bead stopper springs

These little gadgets are ideal for stopping beads falling off the end of the thread or wire (see page 112). There are several sizes available, but the small springs are easier to work around. You can use a stop bead instead (see page 112).

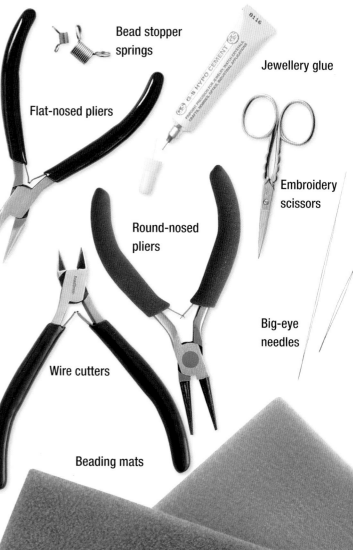

Bead stopper springs

Jewellery glue

Flat-nosed pliers

Embroidery scissors

Round-nosed pliers

Big-eye needles

Wire cutters

Beading mats

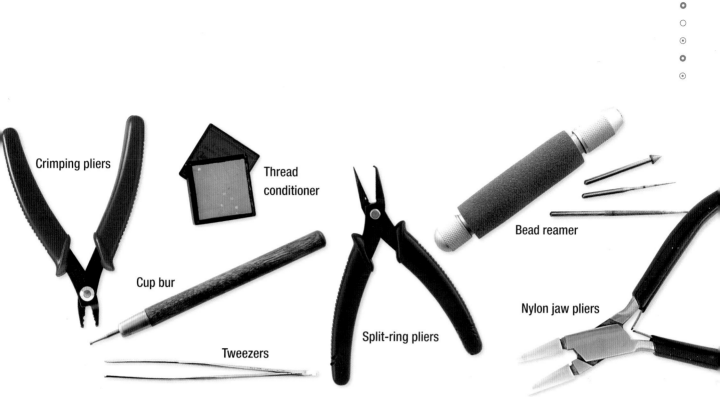

Crimping pliers

Thread conditioner

Cup bur

Tweezers

Split-ring pliers

Bead reamer

Nylon jaw pliers

Big-eye needles

Two very fine needles are soldered together at each end to make a needle with a long eye. These needles are ideal for threading thicker yarns and are available in several sizes.

Jewellery glue

This is a clear-drying glue that doesn't harden completely and so maintains the flexibility of the stringing material while holding the bead or knot secure.

Other tools and equipment

The following items while not essential are worth investing in over time, as they will make the tasks involved in jewellery making easier, and will also help you to achieve a more professional result.

Bead reamer

Most bead reamer tools have several different heads encrusted with fine diamond powder so that you can open out bead holes. This tool is ideal for enlarging the occasionally encountered undersized hole in strings of pearls or other semi-precious stones (see page 14).

Crimping pliers

If you plan to use crimps regularly, crimping pliers will produce a more professional finish than flat-nosed pliers. The latter simply flatten the crimp, while crimping pliers put a dent in one side

of the crimp and then you use the pliers to squeeze the bend crimp to make a neat, rounded tube shape (see pages 116). The pliers come in three sizes to suit different sizes of crimp.

Cup bur

This tool is useful for rounding off the ends of wires, especially when making your own earring wires and other fastenings.

Nylon jaw pliers

Available either as flat- or round-nosed, these specialist tools are useful for straightening wire and for working with very soft aluminium wires so that they don't get damaged.

Split-ring pliers

Split rings are notoriously difficult to open, so if you use them regularly, consider buying these pliers, which have a special tip to open the ring so that you can attach a finding.

Thread conditioners

These are often used to prepare thread for bead stitching. They reduce the amount of friction as the thread is pulled through beads and makes it less prone to tangling, which in turn helps to prolong the life of beaded fabric.

Tweezers

Fine pointed tweezers are useful if you need to untie knots and also for picking up individual small beads from a beading mat or a dish of beads.

Tools of the Trade

Bead spinner

If you are making a multi-strand necklace, this tool will speed up the process considerably. It also makes it easy to mix beads to create a random effect. Larger models are easier to use and will work with fairly small quantities of beads. See page 113 for guidance on how to use.

Bead board

Not essential, but a useful piece of equipment for making necklaces or bracelets. The grooves hold the beads in position so that you can arrange and rearrange them easily, and the curved shape gives a good impression of the finished result. The board is also marked with measurements to make it easy to plan designs and make them the right length. See the chart on page 25 for popular necklace lengths.

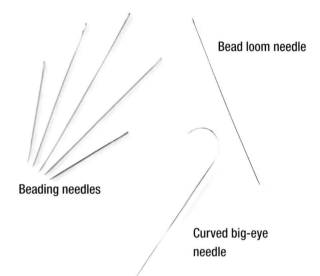

Bead loom needle

Beading needles

Curved big-eye needle

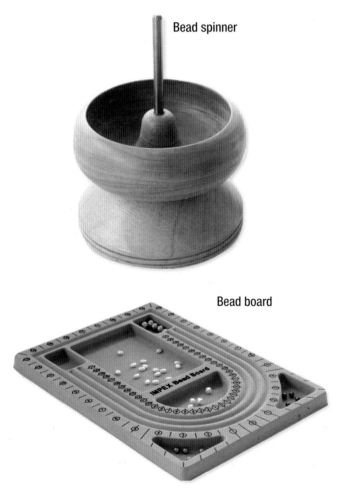

Bead spinner

Bead board

Needles

There are lots of different needles suitable for using with beads and for jewellery making. The type you need will depend on the size of the hole in the bead and the thickness of the thread rather than the bead itself. Follow the guidelines below to help you choose the right needle for the job.

Beading

You can buy bead embroidery needles in short or long lengths. Size 10 or 12 are fine enough for most seed beads, but if you are using petite or size 15 beads (15/0 or 1.3mm) or need to go through seed beads several times, use size 13 or 15. Remember that the finer needles have much smaller holes and you may need to choose a finer thread. Regular quilting needles or sharps are also suitable, which have small, round eyes that are relatively easy to thread. These needles are ideal for embroidery and bead stitches.

Bead loom

These fine, extra-long needles are designed to go through the small holes in seed beads when working on a loom. The length of the needle enables you to go through all the beads at once, but it does make the needle fragile, so keep a stock in case of breakages.

Curved big-eye

These specialist needles are ideal for threading beads using a bead spinner (see above left). The curved shape follows the flow of the beads so that they thread on to the needle quickly.

Tapestry

These large-eye needles, which have a blunt tip, are useful for stringing large beads or when working with yarn or wire.

Twisted wire

Available in several thicknesses, these are ideal for threading through beads with very small holes. The round eye is easy to thread but collapses as it is pulled through the beads. Some silk threads are pre-threaded with a twisted wire needle so that you can string beads with smaller holes, as there is only a single thickness of thread.

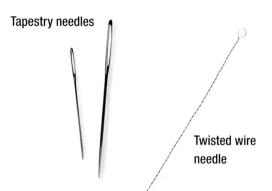

Tapestry needles

Twisted wire needle

⚬ₒₒ∞ₒₒ Bead storage know-how

It is important to store beads carefully so that they are easy to access, don't spill out and can be returned to the container quickly once the work is done. Follow the practical advice below to ensure effective storage.

⊙ Transfer beads, once opened, from their original packaging, such as plastic bags, bubble packs and boxes, to stronger containers.

⊙ Tubes are generally adequate for storage as long as the lid is a good fit, but containers with secure screw tops are more suitable for seed beads and other small beads.

⊙ Label boxes of beads carefully with size, colour and finish, as well as where you bought them.

⊙ Store larger beads in small translucent or clear boxes so that you can see the colours inside, especially useful if you want to mix and match.

⊙ Boxes with a lid and base the same size and shape are particularly useful, as you can tip half the beads into the lid to make it easier to handpick a few.

⊙ Look for inexpensive polythene boxes sold at bead and craft fairs.

Lighting

Good lighting is essential for most beadwork, especially if you are working with small beads or jewellery findings. Even if you don't need to wear spectacles, poor light makes it difficult to see the small holes in the beads and it is hard to open and close jump rings or wire loops accurately. Lamps that direct the light and are fitted with a daylight bulb are the most suitable. A magnifying lamp can be useful for very close work.

Designing your own Necklace

There are plenty of ready-designed necklaces in the book for you to make, but in time you may well be inspired to create your own designs. It is quite easy to string an interesting selection of beads together to make a simple necklace, but a little thought about the style and arrangement will create a superior design.

Planning principles

When making your own necklace, following these basic guidelines to give a structure to your design.

Consider a focal point

First decide if you want to have a focal point, such as a large bead or a cluster of beads, and if so, where to have it. This is usually in the centre, either strung on the bead string or hanging below as a pendant. A focal point at one side is known as a station. Flat beads or embellishments work best in this position and can be extremely flattering close to the collarbone.

Grade your beads

As in colour theory (see page 12), arrange your beads in terms of primary (the main focus of the necklace and usually the most expensive), secondary (for framing and enhancing the primary beads) and tertiary elements (for filling the gaps in between, usually the least expensive). Lay the beads out on a beading mat, or better still, use a bead board (see opposite), as you can then arrange the beads in stages and build up the design knowing that it is going to be the right length.

Experiment with elements

Play around with the sizes and colours of your beads for a while to get everything absolutely right before you begin stringing.

Using a bead board

1 Decide on the length of your necklace and arrange the primary or focus beads on the bead board. This arrangement shows a symmetrical necklace.

2 Place the secondary beads either side of the focus beads. Choose beads that frame and enhance the primary beads so that they are still the main focus.

3 Add tertiary beads to fill the strands. You can use slightly larger beads on the lower half of the necklace, then similar smaller beads to fill up to the fastening.

Lengths of necklace

These are standard necklace lengths, and each necklace design in the book is designated accordingly, but do take into account the height of the person and their body shape and adjust if necessary. The lengths of the necklace projects can easily be adjusted to make alternative styles. Necklaces shorter than 61cm (24in) require a fastening, unless strung on elastic.

Choker: 36–41cm (14–16in), depending on neck measurement
Pendant: 46cm (18in)
Matinee: 51–61cm (20–24in)
Opera: 71–81cm (28–32in)
Rope: 101–114cm (40–45in)
Lariat: over 114cm (45in)

Multi-strand designs

Necklaces with more than one strand need a little forward planning to work out the best method of construction. You can opt for keeping all the strands the same length, or making them graduated in length.

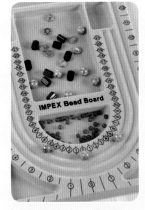

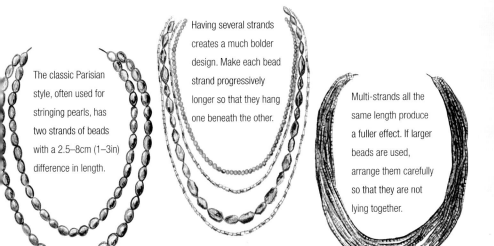

The classic Parisian style, often used for stringing pearls, has two strands of beads with a 2.5–8cm (1–3in) difference in length.

Having several strands creates a much bolder design. Make each bead strand progressively longer so that they hang one beneath the other.

Multi-strands all the same length produce a fuller effect. If larger beads are used, arrange them carefully so that they are not lying together.

Single-Strand Necklace

This may be one of the simplest of styles, yet the variety of designs you can create is infinite. Simply thread your beads on to a string so that they sit side by side, or create a gap between the beads by knotting the string or adding spacers.

Knotting prevents the beads from rubbing together and getting damaged, and also acts as a safety feature, ensuring that the beads will not all fall off if the thread breaks. Spacers are rings or small beads that are practical as well as pretty, and allow larger beads to sit in a gentler curve. Pearls and other semi-precious beads that are used in the Perfect Pearls necklace are usually strung with a knot between each bead for maximum security.

Lovely Lampwork: formal-style necklaces, where beads are usually graduated and arranged in a regular design, can be anything but formal. This fresh and funky necklace would look equally stunning with a casual T-shirt or a summer dress.

Juicy Mosaic: they may appear to be random, but mosaic designs can take as much planning as a symmetrical design. Here, chunky beads are interspersed with smaller beads and spacers to enable the necklace to hang in a softer curve.

Shell Ring Surprise: these gorgeous shell rings were an impulse buy that inspired this contemporary design. Seed beads space the round beads evenly so that they appear to float, and cleverly hide the single strand of bead stringing wire that runs throughout the centre.

Pebble Dangles: for this beautiful design, headpin dangles are slotted in between beads that have been strung on two lengths of bead stringing wire. This holds the dangles firmly in place so that they lie perpendicular to the necklace.

Bead Creative

- When working with pearls, try stringing with a thicker thread to make larger, more decorative knots.
- Add a few headpin dangles (see page 31) in the middle of the necklace, or all the way around for a bolder design.
- Use a bead board to arrange your beads symmetrically and achieve the perfect look before stringing them together (see page 25).

Perfect Pearls: the classic pearl string is the most iconic ❯ *of all of the single-strand designs. For a contemporary take on the knotted pearl necklace, white turquoise beads are alternated with large white pearls strung on thick, natural white silk. The Pearl Drop Earrings (see page 29) complement this simple design for a coordinated look.*

Perfect Pearls

YOU WILL NEED

⊙ 16 round pearls in white, 10mm ⊙ 15 flat, round white turquoise beads, 20mm
⊙ Natural silk cord with in-built needle, 2m (2⅛yd) of no. 10 (0.9mm) ⊙ 2 silver-plated
clamshell calottes ⊙ Silver-plated jump ring (optional) ⊙ Silver-plated necklace clasp
⊙ Tapestry needle ⊙ Basic tool kit (see pages 20–21)

1

You can use a thicker silk cord for stringing the beads if it is purchased with a needle already attached.

2 Tie a loose overhand knot (see page 124) on the silk cord just below the calotte. Use a tapestry needle to guide the knot down to the calotte and pull tight so that the knot is sitting snugly beside it.

2

1 Pick up a clamshell calotte on the silk cord using the in-built needle and drop it down so that the open side is towards the other end of the cord. Tie a figure-of-eight knot (see page 124) on the end, apply a dot of jewellery glue to secure and trim the tail. Use flat-nosed pliers to close the calotte.

Clamshell calottes, which have a hole in the hinge, are more secure than calottes with a side hole.

3

3 Pick up a pearl and drop it down so that it is beside the overhand knot. Tie a second overhand knot and use a tapestry needle to move it down next to the pearl to secure it.

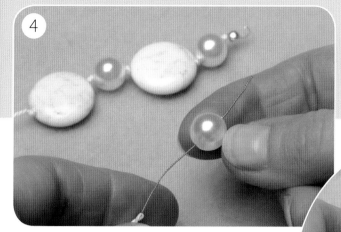

4

MATINEE LENGTH
(see page 25)

4 Pick up a white turquoise bead and tie a third overhand knot. Continue adding pearls and turquoise beads alternately, tying an overhand knot between each bead to ensure that there are no gaps between the beads and knots.

5

5 Tie an overhand knot after the last pearl. Pick up a calotte so that the open end is towards the needle. Tie a figure-of-eight knot and manoeuvre it so that it is inside the calotte with the bead cord taut through the beads. Glue and trim the knot and then close the calotte.

6

6 Open the calotte ring with flat-nosed pliers or use a jump ring to attach the necklace fastening at one end (see page 120). Attach the other two ends of the necklace together using the fastening.

Pearl Drop Earrings

YOU WILL NEED

⊙ Pearls in white: 2 10mm, 2 8mm, 2 6mm and 4 3mm ⊙ 2 flat, round white turquoise beads, 20mm ⊙ 2 silver-plated headpins, 7cm (2¾in) ⊙ 2 silver-plated earring wires ⊙ Basic tool kit (see pages 20–21)

To make these earrings extra special, look out for fancy headpins with a ball or a decorative end.

These graduated earrings are easy to make and are a great way to use up any leftover beads and pearls. The beads are simply slotted on to a silver-plated headpin and a loop is made at the end to attach the earring wire.

Begin by picking up a 3mm pearl, and then add a white turquoise bead. Continue adding the other pearls one at a time, from the largest to the smallest. Trim the end of the headpin to 7mm (⅜in), bend it over using flat-nosed pliers and then use round-nosed pliers to rotate the end around to form a loop (see page 118). Open the loop of an earring wire with flat-nosed pliers (see page 119), attach the earring and close the loop. Make a second earring to match.

Pebble Dangles

YOU WILL NEED

⊙ 16 drop beads in purple, 17mm ⊙ 5g of size 10 triangle beads, colour-lined in purple ⊙ 45 acrylic metal-effect beads, 5mm ⊙ 15 pebble beads in purple, 24mm ⊙ 7-strand bead stringing wire, 0.45mm (26swg) ⊙ 30 silver-plated headpins, 5cm (2in) ⊙ Crimp necklace fastening ⊙ Basic tool kit (see pages 20–21)

CHOKER LENGTH
(see page 25)

1 Cut two 76cm (30in) pieces of bead stringing wire. Pick up a drop bead and two triangle beads on to the wire and repeat this pattern until there are 16 drop beads. Attach a bead stopper spring to each end of the wires (see page 112), allowing space between the drop beads so that they are fairly loose.

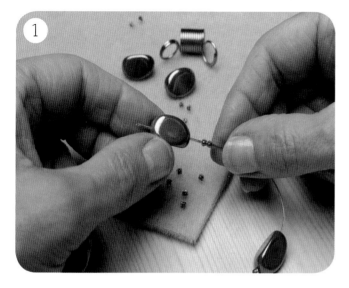

2 Pick up a triangle bead, two metal-effect beads, another triangle bead and a pebble bead on to a headpin. Bend the headpin over at a right angle and use wire cutters to trim the headpin to 7mm (³⁄₈in). Use round-nosed pliers to create a loop on the end (see page 118). On the second headpin, pick up a triangle bead, a metal-effect bead and another triangle bead, then make a loop on the end as before. Repeat with the remaining headpins.

3 Join the two headpin dangles together (see page 118). Separate the bead stringing wire between two triangle beads and slot in the longer headpin dangle so that the wire is between the two metal-effect beads. Repeat so that there is a dangle between each pair of triangles. Attach a crimp necklace fastening to both ends (see page 114).

To get an alternative look in half the time, just add a few dangles in the middle of the necklace.

Shell Ring Surprise

YOU WILL NEED

⊙ 5g of size 8 lined crystal seed beads in dark peach ⊙ 11 shell rings in white, 30mm ⊙ 11 iridescent glass pearls in pastel shades, 12mm ⊙ Bead stringing wire ⊙ Organza ribbon in four pastel shades, 50cm x 1cm (20in x ½in) of each

⊙ 2 round crimps, size 0 ⊙ 2 silver-plated clamshell calottes, 12mm

⊙ Tapestry needle ⊙ Basic tool kit (see pages 20–21)

CHOKER LENGTH (see page 25)

* Pick up two seed beads on bead stringing wire. Feed the end through the hole on one side of a shell ring. Pick up two seed beads, a glass pearl and another two seed beads. Feed the end through the hole at the other side. Repeat from * until all of the large beads are added. Pick up two more seed beads. Add a crimp on each end, then add the clamshell calottes with the hinge end next to the crimps. Fold the wire over the middle of two ribbon lengths and take the wire back through the hole in the clamshell, the crimp and the two seed beads. Pull taut and squeeze the crimp to secure (see page 116). Repeat at the other end, making sure the wire is taut. Tie the ribbons in an overhand knot (see page 124), use a tapestry needle to work it down inside the clamshell and use flat-nosed pliers to close.

Juicy Mosaic

YOU WILL NEED

⊙ Selection of 12 beads in red, yellow and orange, 15–25mm ⊙ 2 flat disc beads in yellow, 30mm ⊙ 7 wood beads in orange, 10mm ⊙ Ceramic beads in a gold finish, 3 10 x 15mm and 3 10 x 20mm ⊙ 52 gold-plated solid rings, 6mm ⊙ Size 4 bead string ⊙ 2 gold-plated bell end cones, 8mm ⊙ Gold-plated toggle fastening ⊙ Basic tool kit (see pages 20–21)

MATINEE LENGTH (see page 25)

Lay the large beads out on a beading mat with a 1cm (½in) gap between them. Arrange the beads so that the larger focus beads are towards the centre and different colours are balanced evenly along the length. Place an orange wood bead in every second gap and alternate the ceramic beads in the other gaps. Cut two 76cm (30in) lengths of bead string and begin threading with a big-eye needle, picking up two solid rings between each bead. Pick up an end cone and take the thread through the ring on the toggle fastening, then back through the end cone. Tie two half-hitch knots (see page 124) before the next bead and apply a drop of jewellery glue. Take the thread through another bead, tie the knots again and secure with glue. Pass the thread through one more bead and trim. Finish the other end in the same way, making sure that the thread is taut before you trim the end.

Lovely Lampwork

YOU WILL NEED

⊙ 5 lampwork beads, 20 x 16mm ⊙ 6 pressed glass beads, 13mm ⊙ 12 round white beads, 10mm ⊙ 12 faceted beads in turquoise, 6mm ⊙ 24 copper spacer beads in a gold finish ⊙ Size 4 bead string ⊙ 2 gold-plated calottes ⊙ Necklace fastening ⊙ Basic tool kit (see pages 20–21)

MATINEE LENGTH (see page 25)

Use a bead board (see page 25) to arrange the lampwork beads. Fill in with the glass beads, then matching smaller beads, adding the copper spacers in between. Cut two 76cm (30in) lengths of bead string and attach a bead stopper to one end (see page 112) and a big-eye needle to the other. Pick up the beads in order, then a calotte, hinge end first. Secure with a figure-of-eight knot (see page 124). Add a drop of glue, trim and close the calotte (see page 114). Repeat at the other end, making sure the thread is taut. Attach a fastening to each calotte.

Pendant

Crazy Paving: sometimes a piece of jewellery takes a leap forward when you come across two elements that match in colour and pattern exactly. This simple design really works because the bead is the same size as the hole in the pendant.

We think of a pendant as a type of necklace, but this Old French word actually refers to the ornament that hangs from it. The necklace style goes back to ancient times when it was a symbol of wealth or represented the religious beliefs or tribal status of the wearer. A pendant can be simply strung on a plain thong or cord, or attached to a necklace. Anne Boleyn, one of Henry VIII's wives, wore a pendant suspended from a pearl necklace, and Pretty in Pink on the right is a modern version. Pendants usually have a hole at the top, but you can explore other innovative approaches like using a large ring to suspend a collection of smaller beads and charms, as in the jadeite bangle design opposite.

Copper Leaves: ring the changes by using chain rather than thong or cord to hang a pendant. Carry the theme to the pendant itself by embellishing a short length of chain with beads and leaf charms. Copper has an aged appearance that works well with the peach and warm-toned beads.

Pretty in Pink: this stunning pink stone pendant would have looked rather lost simply strung on the cord, but chunky semi-precious faceted beads, silver-plated jump rings and sparkly miracle beads add interest and texture, creating an effectively balanced design.

Chunky Charm: This giant bead link, made from chunky beads, is attached to a solid ring that is large enough to feed a toggle bar through. If you attach a toggle bar to both ends of the hanging cord, you can pass it through the solid ring to shorten the necklace to make a choker-style necklace.

Bead Creative

○ Try hanging pendants from different stringing materials such as ribbon, strings of seed beads or chain.

○ Match the colour of the stringing material to the pendant for a coordinated look.

○ Pendants are the most eclectic of necklace styles, so be brave and use unusual beads and other knick-knacks to create the design.

Jadeite Delight: a jadeite bangle makes an unusual ❯ *centrepiece for a pendant. Pick up the dark veining in one of the bead colours and then add complementary-coloured beads to create a stunning design. Antique silver charms add the finishing touch. Use the same techniques to make the Clustered Berries Ring (see page 39) and create a parure (matching jewellery set).*

Jadeite Delight

YOU WILL NEED

⊙ Jadeite bangle, 50mm ⊙ 2 antique silver washer-style spacers, 6mm ⊙ Selection of beads in pink/wine, 6–12mm ⊙ Selection of beads in blue/green, 3–12mm ⊙ 4 antique silver tube beads, 3 x 8mm ⊙ Antique silver butterfly and dragonfly charms

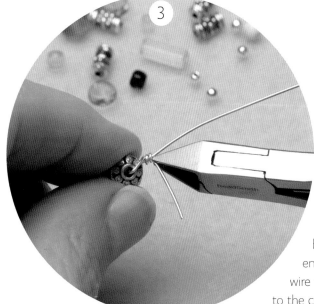

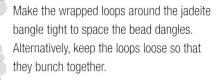

Make the wrapped loops around the jadeite bangle tight to space the bead dangles. Alternatively, keep the loops loose so that they bunch together.

1 To make a wrapped-loop bead dangle, pick up a few beads on a headpin. Hold the headpin near the tip of a pair of snipe-nosed pliers and bend the wire over at right angles about 3mm (⅛in) above the top bead.

2 Curl the rest of the headpin around the jadeite bangle to form a loop. Using flat-nosed pliers, wind the wire around the stem of the headpin about three times (see page 119). Trim the end of the tail close to the coil.

3 To make a bead dangle with wrapped loops at both ends, pick up a washer-style spacer or a leaf bead on the end of a length of the wire, bend the wire back on itself about 2.5cm (1in) from the end and wrap the short tail around the main wire two or three times. Trim the tail close to the coil.

⊙ Resin leaf in burgundy, 12 x 15mm ⊙ 6 silver-plated small round beads ⊙ Waxed cord, 1m (39in) of 2mm ⊙ 5 silver-plated headpins, 7cm (2¾in) ⊙ Silver-plated wire, 0.6mm (24swg) ⊙ 2 silver-plated jump rings ⊙ Basic tool kit (see pages 20–21)

PENDANT LENGTH
(see page 25)

4 Pick up a selection of beads on the wire, then bend the wire at right angles 3mm (⅛in) above the last bead.

5 Wrap the wire around the jadeite bangle and then wrap the tail two or three times around the straight section. Trim the tail close to the coil. Make about seven different wrapped-loop bead dangles in total.

6 To make a charm dangle, make a loop on the end of a length of wire (see page 118). Pick up a selection of beads and then follow Steps 4-5 to attach it to the jadeite bangle with a wrapped loop.

Jadeite Delight

7 Open the loop with flat-nosed pliers, then attach the butterfly charm and close the loop again (see page 118). Make a second charm dangle and attach the dragonfly to the loop in the same way. Repeat with the resin leaf.

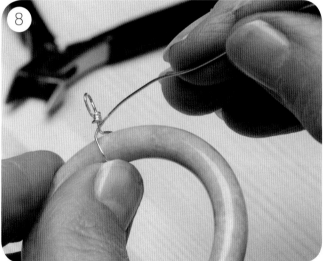

8 To hang the pendant, make a wrapped loop at the end of a length of wire. Bend the wire over 3mm (⅛in) below the coil and wrap the long tail around the jadeite bangle. Wrap the wire tail around two or three times under the previous coil to secure the wire, then trim the end.

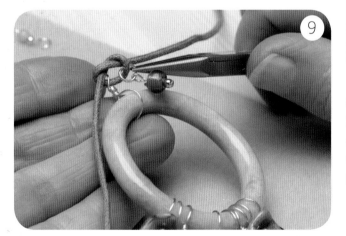

9 Tie the waxed cord through the wrapped pendant loop. Make two bead dangles using headpins, picking up a small silver-plated bead and then either a small pink or a small green bead and finishing with a loop (see page 118). Attach these to the cord knot with jump rings (see page 120).

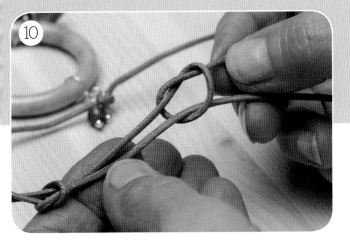

For a more decorative fastening, add a bead to each cord tail, tie an overhand knot after the beads and trim the tail (see Pretty in Pink, page 41).

10 To fasten the necklace so that it can be adjusted, overlap the ends by 15cm (6in). Tie each end over the other cord using an overhand knot (see page 124). Pull the knots away from each other to shorten the cord length.

Clustered Berries Ring

YOU WILL NEED

⊙ Silver-plated ring with 10 wire loops ⊙ Approx. 30 silver-plated round beads, 3mm ⊙ 18 metal-lined beads in pink, 6mm ⊙ 3 flower drops in pink, 12mm ⊙ 4 antique silver tube beads, 3 x 8mm ⊙ 4 antique silver washer-style spacers, 6mm ⊙ 30 silver-plated headpins ⊙ Basic tool kit (see pages 20–21)

Cluster rings may look complicated, but are quite easy to make, as they are simply lots of headpin dangles attached to a ready-made looped ring base. Add two or three to each loop of the ring for a chunky effect.

Make bead dangles using the headpins, picking up a small silver bead and then a pink or antique silver bead, as in Step 9 opposite. Open the loop with flat-nosed pliers, attach it to one of the ring loops and close the loop again. Make a few dangles using the washer-style spacers with a wrapped loop at one end and a plain loop for attaching to the ring loops (see pages 118-119). Add the large flower beads towards the middle of the ring base and mix the antique silver beads in with the pink metal-lined beads.

When you put the ring on your finger, the bead dangles will all push together to make a solid cluster.

Cut the cord in half and then attach both pieces with a Lark's head knot to the pendant (see page 124). Thread the bead on to the four strings of cord and drop it down to the pendant (check that you can get the four lengths of cord through the hole in the horn bead before you begin). Separate the strings of cord and attach a thong end to each pair (see page 114). Attach the fastening to the thong ends using jump rings (see page 120).

Crazy Paving

YOU WILL NEED
⊙ Crazed acrylic pendant in white, 6.5cm (2½in) ⊙ Crazed horn bead in white, 2cm (¾in) ⊙ Waxed cotton cord in black, 2m (2⅕yd) of 1mm ⊙ 2 thong ends ⊙ 2 jump rings ⊙ Hook fastening ⊙ Basic tool kit (see pages 20–21)

OPERA LENGTH (see page 25)

Copper Leaves

YOU WILL NEED
⊙ 30 copper round filigree beads, 3mm ⊙ 14 copper round beads, 6mm ⊙ Selection of 4 accent beads in warm tones ⊙ Resin leaf in brown, 1.5 x 2cm ⊙ Brass leaf charm, 4 x 2.5cm ⊙ Copper heart charm, 7mm ⊙ Copper solid ring, 2cm (¾in) ⊙ Copper chain, 1m (39in) of 6mm (¼in) links ⊙ 6 copper jump rings ⊙ 11 copper headpins ⊙ 7 copper eyepins ⊙ Basic tool kit (see pages 20–21)

PENDANT LENGTH (see page 25)

Cut a six-link length of the copper chain and attach the solid ring to one end and the brass leaf charm to the other end with jump rings (see page 120). Make three small bead dangles using copper headpins with a copper filigree bead and a copper round bead (see page 118). Make four other bead dangles using the accent beads and copper filigree beads. Attach all the bead dangles to the chain links, alternating sides to create a balanced effect (see page 121). Attach the resin leaf and heart charm to the solid ring with jump rings. Make 11 bead links with copper eyepins, picking up a filigree bead, a copper round bead and then a filigree bead (see page 118). Cut 10-link lengths of chain and join together with the bead links. Attach each end of the chain to the solid ring with a jump ring.

Pretty in Pink

YOU WILL NEED

⊙ Stone pendant in pink, 6 x 4.5cm ⊙ 12 miracle beads in pink, raspberry and grey, 6mm ⊙ 8 dyed jade faceted beads in pink, 12 x 15mm ⊙ Waxed cotton cord in white, 1m (39in) of 1mm ⊙ 36 silver-plated jump rings, 5mm ⊙ Basic tool kit (see pages 20–21)

CHOKER LENGTH (see page 25)

Use a Lark's head knot (see page 124) to attach the centre of the cord to the pink pendant. Pick up two jump rings on each end, then a miracle bead. Add another two jump rings and a faceted bead to each length of cord. Continue adding small and large beads with jump rings in between, mixing the colours of the small beads as you go. Once you have added five small beads on each side, tie an overhand knot (see page 124). Follow Step 10 on page 39 to fasten the necklace. Add a miracle bead to each tail, then tie an overhand knot and trim the tail. Pull the beads to adjust the cord length.

Make a loop on one end of the wire using round-nosed pliers (see page 118). Pick up the first four beads in the order below, ending with the blue ceramic bead – pick up size 6 or similar seed beads to fill the larger bead holes so the big beads sit centrally on the wire. Add the small silver-plated round bead to stabilize the larger bead, then trim the wire to 1.5cm (5/8 in). Bend the end at right angles and form into a loop that will fit around the solid ring using round-nosed pliers. Attach the ring and then the heart charm to the other end. Attach the thong to the ring with a Lark's head knot (see page 124) and finish with thong ends and a fastening for a pendant length, or, so that you can adjust to a choker length, secure ends in an end bar (adding a little glue for extra security) and attach the toggle bar with a jump ring.

Chunky Charm

YOU WILL NEED

⊙ Pandora bead, 13mm x 7mm ⊙ Ceramic crinkly bead in a silver finish, 17mm ⊙ Ceramic flat spacer bead in a silver finish, 17mm ⊙ Ceramic bead in blue, 23 x 20mm ⊙ Size 6 or similar seed beads, for filling ⊙ Silver-plated round bead, 6mm ⊙ Silver-plated solid ring, 16mm ⊙ Silver-plated filigree heart charm, 25mm ⊙ Silver-plated wire, 12cm (4¾in) of 1.2mm (18swg) ⊙ Leather thong, 76cm (30in) ⊙ Silver-plated end bar, 6mm ⊙ Silver-plated jump ring ⊙ Silver-plated toggle bar ⊙ Basic tool kit (see pages 20–21)

PENDANT LENGTH or CHOKER LENGTH when shortened with toggle bar (see page 25)

Multi-Strand Necklace

The sumptuous strings of beads hanging in a bead shop are so seductive that you just have to run your fingers through the beads to make them swish and sway. This is one reason why multi-strand necklaces are so popular – they look so opulent. Of course, you don't have to use pre-strung beads; it is great fun mixing your own selection of beads and threading them on to string. Many people find it quite relaxing stringing beads by hand from a beading mat, but a bead spinner (see page 22) is a great time-saver, especially for seed beads. Remember to use two strands of strong thread for each string and take extra care securing the ends, as there are a lot of beads to spill should the thread break!

Shimmering Swirl: this eye-catching design features a particular type of seed bead called a papillon because it resembles butterfly wings. These are strung with seed beads in between to produce an exciting textural effect. End bar fastenings are used to keep the strands separate, which are then wrapped with an elasticated strand of seed beads to create a focal knot-like feature.

Delightful Discs: these donut beads are generally used individually as a pendant, but as they are not expensive, five or seven donuts look absolutely stunning strung together with several strands of toning seed beads. You can make the multi-strands longer or shorter to vary the design.

Braiding in Bronze: this necklace is easier to make than it may appear, as it simply comprises parallel bead strands that are secured at each end and then plaited (braided). For an alternative look, you can just slide the pendant bead off the plaited strand.

Bead Creative

- Use pre-strung beads to make a quick and easy multi-strand necklace.
- Fill one or two strands with larger beads, or try adding some big beads between the seed beads for a completely different look.
- Use spacer bars to keep the bead strands separate and finish the necklace with end bar fastenings.

Horn of Plenty: seed beads have been mixed with focal beads of cracked horn, ceramic and silver in a restricted colour palette to make a bold contemporary necklace. The quality of this necklace depends on the beads you use, so choose small triangle and cylinder beads with a matt or metallic finish to mix with inexpensive silver-lined seed beads for the strands. Use the same elements to make a matching bracelet, stringing the large beads on elastic cord adjoining the strands (see page 47).

Horn of Plenty

YOU WILL NEED

⊙ 15g of cylinder beads in mixed matt greys and clear off-white lined ⊙ 5g of size 11 Toho triangle beads in matt grey ⊙ 20g of size 9 seed beads in silver-lined transparent grey ⊙ 2 ceramic round beads in brown, 20mm ⊙ 2 cracked horn round beads in cream, 15 x 12mm ⊙ 2 antique silver round beads, 8mm ⊙ 3 round beads in matt

1 Mix the cylinder, triangle and seed beads together on a beading mat until you are happy with the colour mix, then tip into a bead spinner.

2 Working off the reel of braided thread and using a curved big-eye needle, pick up 25cm (10in) of beads from the bead spinner (see page 113). Cut the thread, leaving 10cm (4in) tails at each end. Make 15 beaded strands in total. For a fuller-effect necklace, you can add more strands at this stage.

Make sure that you secure the beaded strands with bead stopper springs (see page 112) so that the beads don't fall off as you work.

3 Tie the threads together at one end using an overhand knot (see page 124). Apply a drop of jewellery glue over the knot and leave to dry. Trim the thread ends.

grey, 6mm ⊙ Cracked horn long bead in cream, 50 x 15mm ⊙ Antique silver round bead, 18mm ⊙ Braided thread, size B ⊙ 2 tubular crimps, 3 x 2mm ⊙ 2 clamshell calottes ⊙ Silver-plated jump ring (optional) ⊙ Necklace fastening ⊙ Bead spinner ⊙ Curved big-eye needle ⊙ Basic tool kit (see pages 20–21)

MATINEE LENGTH
(see page 25)

4

4 Cut two 1m (39in) lengths of beading thread and pass through the middle of the beaded strands until the beads are in the centre of the threads. Tie the threads in a reef (square) knot (see page 124). Repeat Steps 3 and 4 at the other end of the beaded strands.

5

5 Thread one set of four ends into a big-eye needle and pick up a ceramic brown bead, a cracked horn round bead, a small antique silver bead and a grey round bead.

6

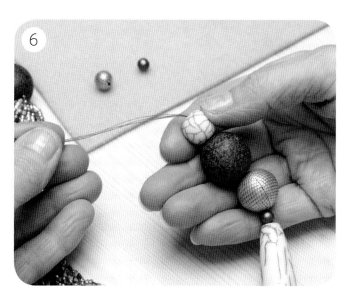

6 At the other end of the beaded strands, pick up the cracked horn long bead, a grey round bead, the large antique silver bead, a ceramic brown bead, cracked horn round bead, small antique silver bead and grey round bead.

Horn of Plenty

7 Thread a single thread on to the curved big-eye needle and pick up 8cm (3in) of seed beads from the bead spinner. Repeat on all the thread ends to create four beaded strands at each end, securing the beads on each strand with a bead stopper spring.

8 Feed one set of thread ends through the hole in a clamshell calotte. Tie the threads in a reef (square) knot, taking care to keep the bead strands taut against the outside of the clamshell calotte.

9 Repeat at the other end of the necklace and add a drop of jewellery glue to each knot. Trim the ends and close the calottes with flat-nosed pliers.

10

10 Attach the calottes to a necklace fastening. Depending on the style of the fastening, you may need to add a jump ring as a spacer so that the end bar goes through the hoop.

You can string the seed beads on to fine elastic thread instead and hide the knot inside one of the larger beads.

Hundreds and Thousands Bracelet

YOU WILL NEED
⊙ 5g of size 9 seed beads in silver-lined transparent grey ⊙ 5g of cylinder beads in mixed matt greys and clear off-white lined ⊙ 5g of size 11 Toho triangle beads in matt grey ⊙ Antique silver round bead, 18mm ⊙ 2 cracked horn round beads in cream, 15 x 12mm ⊙ Ceramic round bead in brown, 20mm ⊙ Size 8 bead thread in smoke ⊙ Elastic cord in black, 25cm (10in) of 1mm ⊙ Organza ribbon in cream, 30cm (12in) each of 6mm and 9mm ⊙ Bead spinner ⊙ Curved big-eye needle ⊙ Basic tool kit (see pages 20–21)

Mix the small beads in a bead spinner and string 15 15cm (6in) lengths of beads on the bead thread (see page 113), leaving an 8cm (3in) tail at each end. Lay the beaded strands in a bundle and tie each end in an overhand knot (see page 124) about 6mm (¼in) from the beads. Trim the tails and put a drop of jewellery glue on the knots to secure. Loop the elastic cord through the middle of the bead strands at one end, then feed both ends through the antique silver bead and tug to pull the knot inside the bead. Take both ends through a cracked horn bead, then take a single tail through the brown bead and other cracked horn bead. Loop the elastic through the other end of the beaded strands and back through the last two beads. Pull tight, then tie the cord with a reef (square) knot (see page 124) and trim the ends. Cut the ribbons into three and tie in pairs between the beads.

Shimmering Swirl

YOU WILL NEED
⊙ 25g of size 9 seed beads in brown AB ⊙ 35g each of papillon beads
in champagne gold, brilliant copper and brilliant gold, 3.2 x 6.5mm
⊙ Size D bead thread ⊙ Elastic thread ⊙ 2 antique silver
five-hole end bars ⊙ Antique silver hook fastening
⊙ Basic tool kit (see pages 20–21)

LARIAT LENGTH (see page 25)

Pour beads on to a
beading mat. Threading on to
the bead thread straight off the reel,
pick up a seed bead, then a papillon bead, and
continue in the same way, changing the colour of the
papillon each time, but pick up two of the same colour
occasionally to create a random look. Make three 90cm
(35½in) beaded strands. Thread two 90cm (35½in) strands
of seed beads. Tie each of the strands to a five-hole end bar.
Tie the threads to the other end bar, keeping the thread taut.
Secure the thread ends inside the beads with a half-hitch
knot (see page 124) and a drop of jewellery glue. Trim
the ends. String a 75cm (29½in) length of seed beads
on to elastic thread and tie in a circle. Secure
both ends with a half-hitch as before. Twist
the elasticated bead string around
the necklace strands.

Delightful Discs

YOU WILL NEED

⊙ 40g of size 11 seed beads in teal metal iris ⊙ 7 donut pendants in light jade, 40mm (1½in) ⊙ Multifilament or braided thread in green, size B ⊙ Craft wire, 0.6mm (24swg) ⊙ 2 bell end cones ⊙ Hook fastening ⊙ Bead spinner ⊙ Curved big-eye needle ⊙ Basic tool kit (see pages 20–21)

MATINEE LENGTH (see page 25)

Pick up the seed beads on to the reel of thread using a bead spinner and a curved big-eye needle (see page 113). To link the donut beads together, cut off three groups of 45 seed beads, leaving 5cm (2in) of thread at each end. Tie the strands of beads around two donuts using a reef (square) knot (see page 124), then secure the thread ends with a half-hitch knot (see page 124) and a drop of jewellery glue. Tie loops of 22 seed beads between the donuts, securing the threads as before. Join all seven donuts in the same way. Separate six 36cm (14in) strands of seed beads. Loop three through each end donut and tie the ends together. Add a 22-seed bead loop around each bundle and drop down to the end donuts. Secure the threads with wire and attach a bell end cone, making a plain or wrapped loop to attach a necklace fastening (see page 115).

Braiding in Bronze

YOU WILL NEED

⊙ 20g of size 11 seed beads in transparent gold AB ⊙ 10g each of size 8 seed beads in gold-lined gold opal, size 11 in bronze, size 9 in gold-lined brown and size 10 in transparent brown ⊙ Jasper paysage donut square pendant, 43mm (1¾in) ⊙ Multifilament or braided thread in brown, size B ⊙ 2 crimps, size 3 ⊙ 2 bronze bell end cones ⊙ Necklace fastening ⊙ Bead spinner ⊙ Curved big-eye needle ⊙ Basic tool kit (see pages 20–21)

PENDANT LENGTH (see page 25)

Pour the transparent gold AB beads into a bead spinner and string six 40cm (16in) separate lengths (see page 113). Also string six 7.5cm (3in) lengths and put to one side. Add the other beads to the bead spinner and string the same number of lengths in mixed beads. Lay the long strings in a mixed bundle and secure the threads at each end with a large crimp (see page 116). Divide the strands into three bundles of four and begin to plait (braid) the strands from one end. Loop the other end through as you go to take out the plaiting (braiding) that forms below your hands until the whole length is plaited in one direction. Attach the end cones (see page 115), adding jewellery glue for extra security, then attach the necklace fastening. Tie the shorter strands around the pendant using reef (square) knots (see page 124). Secure the tails with a half-hitch knot (see page 124) and a drop of glue.

Bib Necklace

A bib is either a clothes protector for a feeding baby or the top part of a pinafore, apron or dungarees that covers the chest. Both definitions describe the bib style of necklace where a panel of beads is created, usually on a choker length, to hang below the neck. You can create the bib shape in a variety of ways: by joining bead links to make long strands, stringing beads to make a fringe or looping beads in a semicircle. Alternatively, try making a panel of chain maille, the ancient technique of linking metal rings together to make a fabric, which is used to contrasting effect in the eclectic Bohemian Rhapsody design opposite and the minimalist Rings and Things on page 57.

Sea Breeze: a ready-made leather necklace forms the base of this fun necklace designed to look like strands of seaweed swaying with the tide. It features gorgeous blue-green pearls, pressed glass shell-like beads and cute metallic sea shapes, all strung on coloured bead stringing wire.

Love Heart: flat beads rather than round work better for this style of bib necklace. The foil beads - these can be either wrapped in foil or the foil embedded into the clear resin of the bead - are made into bead links that hang one under the other in graduated lengths.

Rings and Things: polyester chain and fabulous coin-shaped silver beads were the starting point for this contemporary bib-style necklace. Although the contrast between the black chain and the subtle silver, crystal and white beads works well, the addition of black beads makes it a much stronger design.

Bead Creative

○ Flat beads such as cabochons, with pre-drilled holes or integrated loops, can be linked with jump rings to make a bib shape.
○ Filigree motifs can be incorporated alongside beads for a completely different look.
○ Use graduated strings of beads or add beads to lengths of chain to create the bib shape.

Bohemian Rhapsody: this necklace bib is formed using a ❯ simple chain maille technique, which involves linking large solid rings with jump rings. A selection of beads are then attached, with the colours carefully mixed, together with some frayed organza ribbon, to create a flamboyant design. Use the same technique to transform a standard watch face with a chain maille strap (see page 55).

Bohemian Rhapsody

YOU WILL NEED

⊙ Selection of large and small beads in bright blue, purple, purple/black and golden yellow, including a focal leaf bead ⊙ 15 gold solid rings, 15mm (⅝in) ⊙ Gunmetal finish chain, 40cm (16in) of 5mm ⊙ Gold-plated wire, 30cm (12in) of 0.6mm (24swg) ⊙ Gold-plated chain, 60cm (24in)

1 To make the decorative chain maille panel, lay five solid rings in a row side by side and four solid rings underneath. Link the two rows of solid rings with jump rings (see page 120), using one ring on the outer rings and two on each of the inner rings of the top row. Each solid ring on the second row is connected to the top row using two jump rings.

2 Add three solid rings for the next row as in Step 1, then a row of two followed by a single ring to make a triangle shape. Finally, except for the top row, link the solid rings horizontally with jump rings. Position the chain maille panel in the middle of the gunmetal chain. Use two jump rings to attach each of the five rings in the top row to the chain.

If you can't find solid rings the correct size, look for decorative chain that can be taken apart and use these rings instead.

3 Make a selection of headpin dangles using a mixture of the different-coloured beads, about five or six in each colour. Thread the beads on to headpins, trim to 7mm (⅜in) and make a plain loop in the top (see page 118).

⊙ Organza ribbon in blue, purple and yellow, 50cm (20in) each of 15mm (⅝in)
⊙ 40 gold-plated jump rings, 5mm ⊙ 20 gold-plated headpins ⊙ Gold-plated
spring-style necklace clasp ⊙ Basic tool kit (see pages 20–21)

MATINEE LENGTH
(see page 25)

4 To attach drop beads to the chain maille, pick a drop bead up on a length of the gold-plated wire and fold the tail back on itself. Make a wrapped loop by winding the tail around the main wire two or three times and trimming the end (see page 119). Trim the wire to 7mm (⅜in) and make a loop with round-nosed pliers (see page 118). Start attaching drop beads around the edge of the chain maille panel, interspersed with the headpin dangles.

5 Continue adding the headpin dangles and drop beads one at a time around the edge of the chain maille panel, mixing sizes, shapes and colours to create a balanced effect. Attach a signature leaf bead at the bottom of the triangle as a focal point.

6 Fill in the centre of the chain maille panel with more headpin dangles and drop beads. Move dangles around if required until you are happy with the spacing, colour and weight of the beads.

Bohemian Rhapsody

7 To achieve a really densely beaded effect, attach a bead to every solid ring and to most of the jump rings too. Finally, attach several dangles to the chain at the top of the panel.

8 Use jump rings to attach the ends of the gunmetal chain about 8cm (3in) down from each end of the length of gold-plated chain.

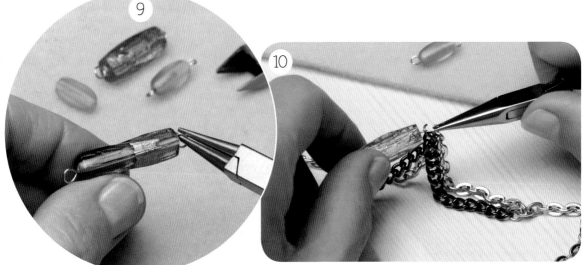

9 Select two long cylinder beads in golden yellow and two in bright blue. Use gold-plated wire to make each bead into a bead link (see page 118).

10 Position one bead link on each side about 6cm (2½in) down from where the two chains join. Open a jump ring and loop the two chains together, then attach one end of a bead link and close the jump ring. Attach the other end of the bead link to the chain in the same way. Repeat for the bead link on the other side. Attach the remaining two bead links further down the chains, leaving a small gap between the beads.

11 Cut 10cm (4in) lengths of organza ribbon in all three colours. Tie the ribbon around the chains above and below the bead links. You can loop the ribbon through the jump rings so that it doesn't slip down.

12 Tie other loops of ribbon to the chain maille panel and then trim in a 'V' shape at each end. Fray the ends of the ribbons slightly to create a bohemian effect.

Run the necklace through your lightly clenched fist to soften the ribbons so that they hang more attractively.

Chain Maille Watch

YOU WILL NEED

⊙ Watch face in a gold finish with end link holes ⊙ Selection of large and small beads in bright blue, purple, purple/black and golden yellow ⊙ 16 gold solid rings, 15mm (⅝in) ⊙ Organza ribbon in blue, purple and yellow, 10cm (4in) of 15mm (⅝in) each ⊙ 25 gold-plated jump rings, 5mm ⊙ 30 gold-plated headpins ⊙ Gold-plated toggle clasp ⊙ Basic tool kit (see pages 20–21)

Cut through two solid rings using wire cutters and open like a jump ring (see page 120). Slot a solid ring into each hole at either end of the watch face. Lay the watch flat and arrange six solid rings in pairs out from each single solid ring. Link each pair with a jump ring and then join the pairs together using single jump rings. Attach a single solid ring at each end with jump rings to make the strap. Tie a piece of ribbon through the first and last pairs of solid rings and trim. Make about 30 headpin or drop bead dangles, following Steps 3-4 on pages 52-53. Attach a bead dangle to each solid ring and each jump ring. Join the round end of the toggle clasp to the top end with a single jump ring. Link two jump rings together and use to attach the end bar at the bottom of the strap.

Sea Breeze

YOU WILL NEED

⊙ Pearls in mixed dark blue, light blue and pale green, approx. 23 6mm, 6 8mm and 9 10mm ⊙ 9 sea-shaped acrylic beads in an antique silver finish, approx. 10mm ⊙ 8 faceted beads in green AB, 12mm ⊙ 8 coin beads in green iridescent, 12mm ⊙ 8 spacer beads in an antique silver finish ⊙ Bead stringing wire in 3 different blue/green shades ⊙ Leather necklace, 40cm (16in) ⊙ 150 silver-plated tube crimps, size 1 ⊙ Paper pricking tool ⊙ Basic tool kit (see pages 20–21)

CHOKER LENGTH (see page 25)

Cut 15 15cm (6in) lengths of the bead stringing wire. Secure a crimp on the end of each strand (see page 116). Pick up a large bead and secure with a second crimp. Secure another crimp about 2cm (¾in) above the last bead. Add the next bead and a crimp. Continue spacing beads, leaving about 2.5cm (1in) at the top. Fill all the strands slightly differently. Using a paper pricking tool, pierce 15 holes spaced 6mm (¼in) apart in the centre of the leather necklace. Attach a crimp on the central strand about 1.5cm (⅝in) from the top. Feed through the centre hole and add a small pearl. Secure with a crimp and trim the wire flush. Add the other strands, varying the gap between the last bead and the leather necklace. Add a crimp above the thong to add height to one or two beads for a random effect.

Love Heart

YOU WILL NEED

⊙ 7 opaque ivory with silver coin beads, 15mm ⊙ 36 silver-plated irregular spacer beads, 6mm ⊙ 3 transparent gold shimmer oval beads, 30 x 15mm ⊙ 2 transparent gold shimmer round beads, 18mm ⊙ 7 ball beads in a silver finish, 3mm ⊙ 6 opaque ivory with silver round beads, 12mm ⊙ Heart charm in a silver finish, 3cm ⊙ Silver-plated wire, 2m (2⅛yd) of 0.6mm (24swg) ⊙ Silver-plated chain, 38cm (15in) of 3mm links ⊙ 7 silver-plated headpins ⊙ Silver-plated hook fastening ⊙ Basic tool kit (see pages 20–21)

CHOKER LENGTH (see page 25)

Make bead links with the coin beads on the wire, adding a spacer bead on either side (see page 118). Make a similar bead link with each of the transparent shimmer beads. For the headpin dangles, pick up a small silver ball, a spacer bead, an opaque ivory round bead and a spacer bead. Bend the tail over and trim the headpin to 7mm (³⁄₈in), then make a loop on the end with round-nosed pliers (see page 118). To make the heart dangle, pick up the heart bead with a silver ball on both sides on a headpin and make a loop as before. Join the bead links and dangles as shown (see page 118). Attach the bead strand with the heart link in the centre of the chain and the others spaced about 2cm (³⁄₄in) apart. Attach a hook fastening to the ends of the chain.

Rings and Things

YOU WILL NEED

⊙ 5 faceted beads in clear, 11mm ⊙ 8 faceted beads in opaque black, 6mm ⊙ 5 ceramic coin beads in a silver finish, 21mm ⊙ 10 silver-finish ball beads, 5mm ⊙ 5 ceramic round beads in iridescent white, 16mm ⊙ 10 silver-plated solid rings, 24mm ⊙ Polyester chain in black, 40cm (16in) ⊙ 20 silver-plated jump rings ⊙ 23 silver-plated headpins ⊙ Silver-plated toggle fastening ⊙ Basic tool kit (see pages 20–21)

CHOKER LENGTH (see page 25)

Arrange the solid rings in two rows of five and join with a single jump ring (see page 120). Centre the polyester chain and join each ring to the chain with a jump ring. Make headpin dangles with all the faceted beads and the silver-finish coin beads (see page 118). Pick up a ball bead either side of a white ceramic bead to make these into headpin dangles too. Attach a silver coin dangle to the five bottom rings (see page 118). Attach each clear faceted bead dangle to five of the solid rings with a jump ring as shown. Attach three of the white ceramic bead dangles through the polyester chain and into the top rings below so that they hang centrally, with the other two attached to the bottom of the top row of rings. Finally, attach a black bead dangle to each of the remaining jump rings. Attach a toggle fastening to the polyester chain with jump rings.

'Y'-Shaped Necklace

This is one of the most flattering necklace styles, drawing attention to the neck, cleavage and décolletage in the most feminine way. The 'Y' shape may be simple, but there are innumerable ways to interpret the design; rosary beads, with a crucifix attached at the tail, is a classic 'Y' style. Rosary necklaces are often made using bead links, an invaluable technique that provided the inspiration for Pearly Queen opposite. The links are handmade from silver-plated craft wire, or you can use sterling silver wire for a really special necklace. Chain is also an ideal material to use, as the three ends can be linked with a jump ring, or simply string a single strand of beads and try out some innovative ways to create the tail of the 'Y' shape.

Domino Effect: a chance find inspired this unusual 'Y'-shaped necklace – a square wooden bead with four pre-drilled holes that create the junction box for the necklace strings. Teaming it with tubular black and starkly contrasting white beads makes for a dramatic design, with the small round beads in between ensuring that the necklace drapes elegantly. If you can't find the appropriate bead, use spacer bars with four holes for a similar effect.

Rock 'n' Roll: the translucent rocks and wheel-shaped ceramic beads featured here perfectly complement each other, and when linked with copper wire and beads, the design really comes together. Use copper eyepins to make the links rather than copper wire, as the eyepins have an antique finish.

Raspberry Rosary: adding lengths of chain between the bead links brings an unexpected twist to this rosary-style necklace. Picking up the colours found in the lampwork beads for the other beads makes for a harmonious design, and the tiny silver filigree caps serve to soften the transition from chain to bead. You could use chain with larger links to create a completely different look.

Bead Creative

o Shorten or lengthen any of these designs so that the 'Y' shape lies anywhere from your neck to your waist.
o Add a large solid metal ring at the centre of the 'Y' on bead link or chain necklaces to create a focal point.
o Mix chain and bead links to make an infinite variety of necklace designs.

Pearly Queen: a beautiful pearl necklace fit for a queen ❯
– the filigree caps look absolutely stunning against the subtle pastel shades of the pearl beads. Look for antique silver leaf charms to add a finishing touch to the fabulous focal pearl cluster. It is easy to adapt the pearl cluster to make a pair of filigree pearl earrings (see page 63).

Pearly Queen

YOU WILL NEED

⊙ Approx. 60 mixed pearls in white, cream, blue and coffee, 6mm ⊙ Pearls, 2 13mm in coffee, 15mm in cream and 15mm in blue ⊙ Approx. 100 silver-plated filigree caps, 6mm ⊙ 4 silver-plated filigree caps, 15mm ⊙ 10 silver-plated leaf beads, 10 x 6mm

1 Trim the wire flush at one end and make a loop with round-nosed pliers. Hold the wire about 6mm (¼in) down from the tip of the jaws to make the loop the same size each time. Reposition the pliers and bend the tail back slightly so that the loop is straightened and looks like an eyepin (see page 118).

2 Pick up a small filigree cap, a small pearl and another filigree cap so that the caps enclose the pearl. Supporting the loop with your finger so that it is held against the filigree cap, bend the wire at right angles and trim to 7mm (⅜in).

Use antique-silver filigree caps to give the necklace an aged appearance.

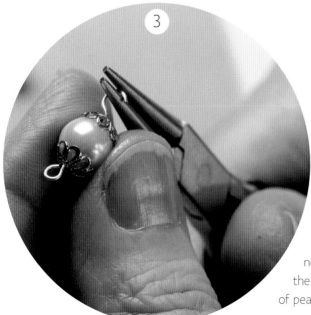

3 Hold the wire at the same point down the pliers as you did in Step 1 and bend round to make a loop with round-nosed pliers (see page 118). Make 38 links in the same way using the four different colours of pearl.

⊙ Silver-plated jewellery wire, 2m (2⅛yd) of 0.6mm (24swg) ⊙ 30 silver-plated
jump rings ⊙ Approx. 25 silver-plated headpins ⊙ Necklace fastening (optional)
⊙ Basic tool kit (see pages 20–21)

MATINEE LENGTH
(see page 25)

4 To join the links, open one end of a
link with flat-nosed pliers by pushing
the loop down. Insert the second link
and close the loop in the opposite way
(see page 118).

5 Join half the links in
one chain and the rest
to make a second
chain. Join the
two lengths by
inserting the
end bead link
loop from
each into a
jump ring.

6 Attach the other jump rings to the first one to make a
simple chain that forms the 'Y' shape of the necklace. See
page 120 for a quick method for making a jump ring chain.

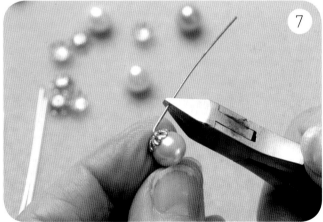

7 Make the remaining pearls into headpin dangles. Pick
up a pearl and then a filigree cap on a headpin. Bend the
end of the headpin at right angles, trim to 7mm (⅜in) and
make into a loop with round-nosed pliers (see page 118).

Pearly Queen

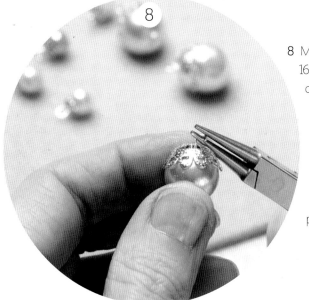

8 Make about 16 small pearl charms and four charms using the larger filigree caps with the large pearls, as in Step 7 on page 61.

You can increase the size of the filigree caps slightly to fit the largest pearls by squeezing between each scallop with wire cutters.

9 Attach the large blue pearl charm to the bottom jump ring in the chain. Attach the other large pearls on alternate sides fairly equally spaced up the jump-ring chain.

10 Attach a small pearl charm to most of the remaining jump rings, alternating the side that the charms are attached so that they hang attractively.

11 Use the remaining jump rings to attach the silver-plated leaves to the jump-ring chain. Again, attach the leaves to alternate sides so that the result is balanced.

12 Check the length of the necklace and add or remove bead links if required. This necklace is almost long enough to go over your head, but it can be easier to attach a necklace fastening to each end. Simply open the last link at each end, insert the fastening and close again.

Pearl Cluster Earrings

YOU WILL NEED

⊙ Approx. 16 pearls in white, cream, blue and coffee, 6mm
⊙ 2 pearls in blue, 15mm ⊙ Approx. 16 silver-plated filigree caps, 6mm ⊙ 2 silver-plated filigree caps, 15mm ⊙ Silver-plated leaf beads, 6 10 x 6mm and 4 12 x 8mm ⊙ 28 silver-plated jump rings, 5mm ⊙ 18 silver-plated headpins ⊙ 2 silver-plated earring wires
⊙ Basic tool kit (see pages 20–21)

Make each of the pearls into a headpin dangle, as follows. Pick up a pearl and then a filigree cap (use the large filigree caps for the large blue pearls) and insert a headpin from the pearl side. Bend the headpin at an angle and trim to 7mm (³⁄₈in). Use round-nosed pliers to make a loop (see page 118). Make two lengths of chain using nine jump rings in each (see page 120). Attach an earring wire to the top of each jump-ring chain (see page 119) and the large blue pearls to the bottom. Beginning at the top ring, attach a pearl charm and a small leaf using another jump ring. Continue down the chain, adding pearl charms to every jump ring, alternating sides, and then attach the remaining leaf charms using jump rings so that they are evenly spaced down the chain.

Change the earring wires to screw or clip fittings to adapt these earrings for wearers without pierced ears.

Domino Effect

YOU WILL NEED

⊙ 28 carved bone round beads in white, 8 x 6mm ⊙ 34 round beads in black, 6mm ⊙ 12 carved bone cylinder beads in white, 25 x 6mm ⊙ 12 wood cylinder beads in white-patterned black, 23 x 5mm ⊙ 14 plain bone cylinder beads in white, 25 x 6mm ⊙ 12 wood cylinder beads in black, 36 x 6mm ⊙ Wood square spacer bead with four holes in black, 25 x 25mm ⊙ Leather thong in black, 2m (2⅙yd) of 1mm ⊙ Basic tool kit (see pages 20–21)

CHOKER LENGTH (see page 25)

Cut the thong in half and tie an overhand knot in one end of each piece (see page 124). Pick up a white carved bone round bead, a black round bead, a white carved bone cylinder bead, a black round bead and a patterned black cylinder bead on each length. Feed the thong through two holes at one side of the spacer bead. Put the same beads used so far to one side. Arrange the remaining long beads in sets of four, alternating between black and white and carved and patterned. Add white bone round beads next to the black cylinder beads and black round beads next to the white cylinder beads. Place the last two white cylinder beads at the top. String the other beads in the same order until you reach the spacer again. Feed the thong through without twisting the strands and pick up the beads set aside in reverse order. Tie the thong off and trim the ends.

○ ⊙ ● ○ ⊙ ● 'Y'-Shaped Necklace

Rock 'n' Roll

YOU WILL NEED

⊙ 6 ice rock beads in pink, 20mm ⊙ 7 ceramic beads in pink glaze, 23 x 7mm
⊙ 32 copper beads, 6mm ⊙ Copper headpin ⊙ 28 copper eyepins, 4.5cm
(1¾in) ⊙ Copper toggle fastening ⊙ Basic tool kit (see pages 20–21)

OPERA LENGTH (see page 25)

Feed the headpin through the largest rock bead, trim the end to 7mm (⅜in) and use round-nosed pliers to make a loop (see page 118). Use the eyepins to make the bead links with the remaining large beads (see page 118). Use eyepins to make links with the small copper beads – you should be able to use the cut-off section to make bead links for half the beads. Join the headpin rock to a copper bead link (see page 118), then add a ceramic bead link, a copper bead link and a rock bead link to make the tail of the 'Y' shape. Attach two copper bead links to the rock bead loop, then add alternate ceramic and rock bead links with copper bead links in between. After the last large beads, join the remaining copper bead links together. Finish the necklace with a toggle fastening.

Raspberry Rosary

YOU WILL NEED

⊙ 10 miracle beads in raspberry, 10mm
⊙ 5 Czech firepolish beads in burgundy, 12mm
⊙ 8 lampwork beads in cream/raspberry/
brown, 12 x 10mm ⊙ 36 silver-plated filigree
caps, 4mm ⊙ Silver-plated wire, 1m (39in) of
0.6mm (24swg) ⊙ Silver-plated chain, 76cm
(30in) of 4mm ⊙ Silver-plated jump ring
⊙ 3 silver-plated headpins ⊙ Basic tool kit
(see pages 20–21)

MATINEE LENGTH (see page 25)

Make five bead links with the wire using a filigree cap either side of a raspberry bead, then a firepolish bead and another raspberry bead with filigree caps (see page 118). Flatten ten filigree caps with flat-nosed pliers and make five lampwork links with these flat caps. Cut nine pieces of chain with ten links. Join two chain pieces to one lampwork link, for the bottom centre of the necklace, then add two sets of bead and lampwork links spaced with chain pieces on either side. Join the two ends with a piece of chain, about 33cm (13in) long, so that the necklace will go over your head. Add the last bead link with a piece of chain to the bottom lampwork link. Cut three pieces of chain, 8, 10 and 12 links in length, and attach to the bottom bead link with a jump ring. Make three lampwork and filigree cap charms with the headpins (see page 118) and attach to the chain pieces to finish.

Collar

Lilac Loops: this elegant seed bead necklace, inspired by a 1930s example, was complicated to design but is actually extremely easy to make. The bead loops are simply added one at a time to a base necklace, gradually increasing and then decreasing the number of beads to create the collar effect.

Miracle Bars: spacer bars are usually fairly insignificant in a necklace design, but these chunky bars of metal are as crucial to this collar design as the subtly silvery beads. Some of the bars are kept parallel and other bars spaced at an angle to create the collar shape.

Captivating Turquoise: short lengths of chain made from black jump rings act as spacers for this classic Egyptian-style collar. The two necklace strands are separated by wire links, alternating between the glorious metal basket beads and mixed turquoise beads. Silver washer-style beads add the finishing touch.

The collar is perhaps the most opulent necklace style because of its sheer abundance of beads and is certainly the one to choose when the fashion trend is more, more, more. Collars look absolutely stunning with a low-cut or off-the-shoulder dress and have a long history, especially where royalty and wealth are concerned. They were especially popular in Egypt at the time of the Pharaohs; Captivating Turquoise on page 75 is a contemporary interpretation. Multiple strings of graduated pearls or crystals are a classic, especially if the necklace is fastened with a luxurious clasp worn at the front rather than nape of the neck to emphasize the collar shape. Alternatively, create dozens of overlapping loops of beads or use spacer bars to form the collar shape.

Bead Creative

- Where possible, begin a collar necklace on the inner strand and arrange beads around your neck to gauge the spacing required on the outer edge.
- Add seed beads, jump rings or washer-style beads to gradually increase the gap between beads.
- Use spacer bars to keep strings of beads separate and lying flat around your neck.

Hot Property: this fabulous necklace can be worn with the decorative clasp at the nape of the neck, at the front or to one side as a focal point. Although the firepolish beads are stunning on their own, the bright orange miracle beads add an extra element of zing and lift this necklace on to a higher plain. Make the matching Fiery Brooch to pin to your bag or jacket (see page 71).

Hot Property

YOU WILL NEED

⊙ Czech firepolish beads, 45 10mm in red, 42 8mm in burgundy, 54 6mm in orange, 26 4mm in orange ⊙ 42 miracle beads in orange, 9mm ⊙ 16 wax pearls in a gold finish, 2.5mm ⊙ 14 metallic-effect round beads in a gold finish, 6mm ⊙ Bead stringing wire ⊙ Gold-plated craft wire, 4mm (8swg) ⊙ 8 gold-plated crimps, size 1 ⊙ Gold-plated filigree fastening ⊙ Basic tool kit (see pages 20–21)

Use bead stopper springs on each strand to keep the beads on the wires while you are making the necklace (see page 112).

1 Cut four 60cm (23½in) lengths of bead stringing wire. String a different firepolish bead and the miracle beads on each length, leaving two red firepolish beads and the 4mm orange firepolish beads to one side.

2 Hold the bead stringing wire that is strung with the largest firepolish beads. Thread a crimp on to the wire and take the end through the last hole in the filigree fastening. Go back through the crimp again. Pull the wire through to leave a 2.5cm (1in) tail.

3 Push the crimp up to the filigree fastening and then compress with crimping pliers (see page 116). Feed the beads over the tail to hide it and adjust the bead stopper springs so that the beads are taut.

4

4 Repeat with each of the other wires, attaching the wires equally spaced along the edge of the filigree fastening. Hide all the tails inside the beads on each strand.

5

5 At the other end of the beads, feed each of the bead stringing wires through the corresponding holes in the other side of the filigree fastening. Secure with small bead stopper springs. Check that the necklace strings hang together around your neck and that the strings are the right length. Adjust if required.

6

6 Remove the bead stringing wire with the smallest firepolish beads from the filigree fastening, then pick up a crimp. Feed the wire through the corresponding hole in the other side of the filigree fastening and then back through the crimp and several beads. Pull up so that the wire and beads are taut. Secure the crimp with pliers as before.

7

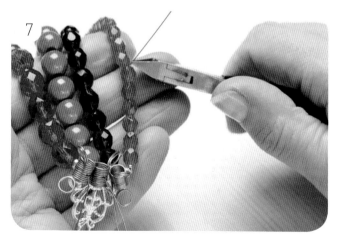

7 Trim the tail with wire cutters, cutting as close to the beads as possible. Repeat with the other bead strings, securing each wire with a crimp and cutting the tail each time.

8 To decorate the filigree fastening, pick up a wax pearl on a 50cm (20in) length of the gold-plated wire, drop it down to the middle and feed both ends through one of the remaining red firepolish beads.

9 Feed the wires through the middle of one side of the filigree fastening, straddling one of the mesh wires. Bring one of the wires up through the filigree fastening near the red firepolish bead.

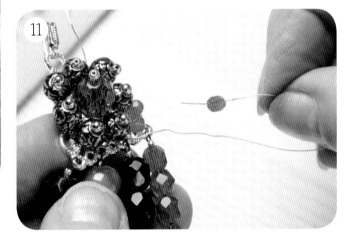

10 Pick up a gold metal-effect bead and a wax pearl. Pass the wire back through the metal-effect bead and the filigree fastening. Continue around the large red firepolish bead, adding a further six metal-effect beads and wax pearls.

11 Bring the gold wire up through the filigree fastening so that you can add small orange firepolish beads around the centre beads. Depending on the shape of your filigree fastening, you can create a circle or, as in this case, a heart shape.

Add the beads to the filigree fastening in an orderly way so that the wire on the reverse is neat and tidy.

12 Feed any wires back between the beads so that there are no sharp edges on the underside to scratch the wearer's neck. Trim any wires to finish. Work the same design on the other side of the fastening and finish in the same way.

Fiery Brooch

YOU WILL NEED

⊙ Gold-plated oval filigree brooch, 4 x 3cm (1½ x 1¼in) ⊙ Czech firepolish beads, 1 10mm in red, 2 8mm in burgundy, 12 6mm in orange and 28 4mm in burgundy ⊙ 6 metallic-effect round beads in a gold finish, 6mm ⊙ 8 wax pearls in a gold finish, 2.5mm ⊙ Gold-plated craft wire, 4mm (8swg) ⊙ Basic tool kit (see pages 20–21)

If you can't find a gold-plated brooch, spray a silver one with gold paint.

Pick up the large red firepolish bead on a 30cm (12in) length of the gold-plated wire and drop it down to the middle. Feed both ends through a gold metallic-effect bead and then pass each end through a separate hole in the middle of the filigree mesh. Take each tail back up through the mesh ready to add a large burgundy firepolish bead either side of the centre bead. Pick up a burgundy bead and a wax pearl on each wire, passing the tail back through the burgundy bead and the mesh. Add three gold metallic-effect beads to fill in on each side in the same way. Attach orange firepolish beads one at a time with the wire to create a ring around the centre beads and then finish with a round of small burgundy beads. Attach the decorated mesh to the brooch back by squeezing the metal lugs down over the mesh to finish.

Lilac Loops

YOU WILL NEED

⊙ 15g of size 6 seed beads in dark peach-lined crystal ⊙ 20g of cube beads in matt light amethyst, 4mm ⊙ 15g of size 11 seed beads in matt antique rose ⊙ 15g of size 8 seed beads in dark peach-lined crystal ⊙ Bead stringing wire, 60cm (24in) ⊙ Waxed nylon bead thread in dusty rose, size A ⊙ 2 crimp ends ⊙ Necklace fastening ⊙ Basic tool kit (see pages 20–21)

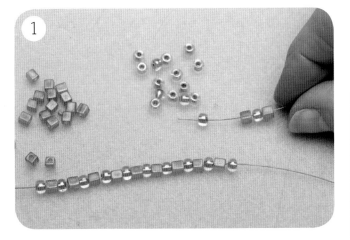

1 Thread size 6 dark peach seed beads and cube beads alternately on to the bead stringing wire until there are 50 seed beads and 49 cube beads. Secure the beads with a small bead stopper spring at each end (see page 112).

CHOKER LENGTH
(see page 25)

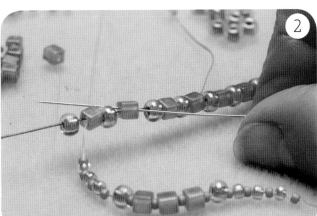

2 Take the needle, threaded with waxed nylon thread, back through an end cube bead, leaving a tail. Picking up a size 11 matt antique rose seed bead either side of every bead, string three size 8 dark peach seed beads, a size 6 dark peach seed bead, three cube beads, a size 6 seed bead and three size 8 seed beads. Take the needle back through the next cube bead along and repeat the same loop.

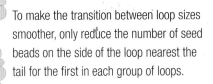

To make the transition between loop sizes smoother, only reduce the number of seed beads on the side of the loop nearest the tail for the first in each group of loops.

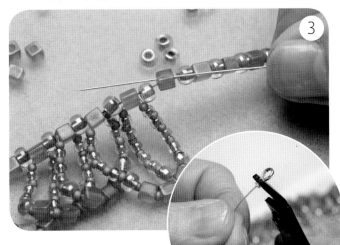

3 Continue adding loops of beads, following the chart on the right, lengthening the loops gradually as you work towards the centre loop. Then follow the chart in reverse, reducing the loop length to make the opposite side of the necklace. If you need to make the necklace longer, add a few more loops at each end before attaching the fastening. Attach a crimp end to each end of the wire (see page 18) and then attach a necklace fastening.

No. of loops	Size 8 seed beads	Size 6 seed beads	Cube beads	Size 6 seed beads	Size 8 seed beads
3	3	1	3	1	3
1	4	1	3	1	4
5	5	1	4	1	5
5	5	1	5	1	5
5	6	1	5	1	6
3	7	1	5	1	7
1	7	1	6	1	7
1	7	1	7	1	7

Miracle Bars

YOU WILL NEED
⊙ 150 miracle beads in off-white, 6mm ⊙ 5g of cylinder beads in galvanized silver ⊙ 105 faceted beads in grey, 6mm ⊙ 14 antique silver spacer bars, 5 x 40mm ⊙ Bead stringing wire, 5 76cm (30in) lengths ⊙ 20 silver-plated crimps, size 1 ⊙ Silver-plated 5-hole necklace fastener ⊙ Basic tool kit (see pages 20–21)

CHOKER LENGTH (see page 25)

String a miracle bead, a cylinder bead, a faceted bead, a cylinder bead and a miracle bead in the middle of one length of wire. Feed the wire on both sides into the top hole of a spacer bar. Add one more miracle bead and cylinder bead to each subsequent string for the remaining spacer bar holes to create a shaped panel. * String three beads plus cylinder beads and a spacer bar as before on each strand on both sides. Then work the shaped panel on both sides. Repeat from * on both sides, then finish with two panels of three beads. Add a spacer bar to both ends. Check that the collar lies flat around your neck. Pick up a bead, five cylinder beads and two crimps on the two centre wires. Pass the wires through the centre holes of the fastening and back through the two crimps. Secure the crimps with crimping pliers (see page 116) and trim the wire. Attach the other wires to the fastening, adding more cylinder beads to keep the two end spacer bars parallel.

Captivating Turquoise

YOU WILL NEED

⊙ 11 antique silver metal beads, 28 x 18mm ⊙ 30g of plastic bead mix in turquoise, 5–10mm ⊙ 36 ceramic tubes in a silver finish, 7 x 5mm ⊙ 16 miracle beads in turquoise, 10mm ⊙ Silver-plated wire, 0.6mm (24swg) ⊙ Bead stringing wire, 2 76cm (30in) lengths ⊙ Satin or velvet ribbon in turquoise, 1m (39in) of 7mm ⊙ 780 black jump rings, 5mm ⊙ 2 silver-plated E-Z crimp ends ⊙ Basic tool kit (see pages 20–21)

OPERA LENGTH (see page 25)

Join all the jump rings into groups of three (see page 120). Make the large silver beads into bead links with the wire (see page 118). Make ten 2.8cm (1¹/₁₆in), two 2.2cm (⁷/₈in) and two 1.8cm (³/₄in) bead links using small turquoise beads and some ceramic tubes. Pick up a large silver bead link on bead stringing wire. * Pick up two sets of jump rings, taking the wire through all the rings, then a bead from the mix and two sets of jump rings. Add a 2.8cm (1¹/₁₆in) bead link and repeat from *. Add a large silver bead link and repeat the whole sequence, adding five silver beads and five 2.8cm (1¹/₁₆in) bead links on each side. On the bottom wire, add two beads from the mix, spaced with two jump ring groups between the bead links. At each end add the beads and jump ring groups to space out the progressively shorter bead links. Attach E-Z crimp ends (see Step 3, page 73) and trim the wire. Thread the ribbon through the loops to secure the necklace.

Lariat

It may not seem very elegant and a far cry from the world of beads, but lariat is another word for lasso, used by cowboys for herding cattle. The original lariat necklace was constructed in exactly the same way as a lasso rope with a loop at one end and the other end finished to prevent it fraying, but now the term encompasses any open-ended necklace. Lariats are unusual in that you can wear the necklace in lots of different ways: draped once or twice around the neck, doubled up to make a shorter style or tied in a knot. To achieve this versatility, the lariat needs to be at least 1m (39in) long.

Flower Fancy: this unusual lariat has scarf clips at each end to be clipped on to the neckline or lapels of your garment. Use pre-strung seed beads to make the necklace in the minimum of time, then decorate the perforated clips with mixed pearls and translucent resin flowers and leaves.

Rustic Charm: many bead shops have trays of individual beads arranged by colour and it is quite easy to pick up a selection of toning beads to make a lariat like this. Plenty of plastic beads have been mixed with the pressed glass and ceramic beads so that it is not too heavy, and the ends finished with large lightweight resin beads.

Chain Reaction: most lariat necklaces are open-ended, but this delicate chain necklace is fastened using a lariat tube and loop set. The loop is attached to one end, but you need to make sure that the beads and chain at the other end will pass through this loop before you attach the tube. If you don't have a lariat loop and tube set, pass the lariat end through one of the large solid rings.

Bead Creative

○ Make lariats as long as you can – a 1.5m (59in) necklace gives you more choice in how it is worn.

○ When stringing lariats, add plastic beads between better quality beads to reduce the weight.

○ Plan a seemingly random necklace carefully so that the colour, size and shape of the beads look balanced along the length.

Twist and Snake: spiral bead techniques are perhaps the ❯ *most suitable bead-stitching methods for necklaces, as they are so strong and secure. This double core spiral mixes quality seed beads, short bugles and double Delica hex beads to make an interestingly textured rope finished with pretty tassels. Use the same technique to make an unusual chain link bracelet (see page 81).*

Twist and Snake

YOU WILL NEED

⊙ 25g each of size 8 double Delica seed beads in cinnamon gold lustre and lined light blue ⊙ 25g of bugles in purple iris matt metal, 3mm ⊙ 15g each of size 11 seed beads in steel blue metallic, light sapphire grey lustre AB and s-l aqua ⊙ 20 glass

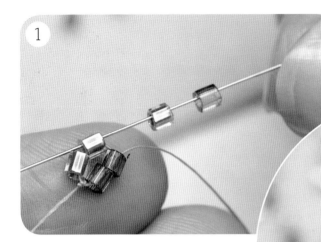

1 Using a 2m (2⅛yd) length of thread with the beading needle, pick up two cinnamon double Delicas and two blue double Delicas, drop them down to 50cm (20in) from the end and tie in a circle. Take the needle through the two cinnamon beads again and add another cinnamon and blue bead. Take the needle through the blue and then the cinnamon beads again ready to add another pair of beads.

2 * Pick up a cinnamon and a blue double Delica and pass the needle down through two of the blue beads already added. Pick up a bugle and take the needle directly across and up through two cinnamon beads. Turn the beading over to the other side.

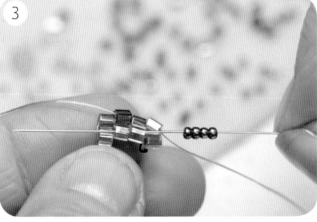

3 Pick up four steel blue seed beads. These will sit diagonally across the block of four Delicas below where the thread is emerging, so count down two blue Delicas and take the needle back up only through these two beads, coming out between the top two blue Delicas.

cylinder beads in assorted colours, 10 x 4mm ⊙ Multifilament thread, size D
⊙ Beading needle ⊙ Basic tool kit (see pages 20–21)

LARIAT LENGTH
(see page 25)

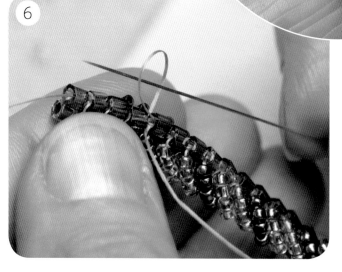

4 Turn the beading over and take the needle across and back through the top cinnamon Delica ready to begin the sequence again. Repeat from * using light sapphire seed beads on the next repeat instead of steel blue and aqua beads on the one after.

Take special care to follow the instructions carefully as you work through the first few steps so that you don't make any mistakes.

5 Repeat the sequence, using the three different colours of seed bead in rotation. Continue working the bead rope until you are ready to join on a new length of thread. Stop when you have about 10cm (4in) of thread left.

6 Thread the needle with a new length of thread and take the needle up through several Delicas to emerge about four Delicas from the end of the bead rope, take the needle behind two threads between the beads and bring it out through the loop of thread to form a half-hitch knot (see page 124). Take the needle through the remaining beads to come out the same bead as the old thread.

Twist and Snake

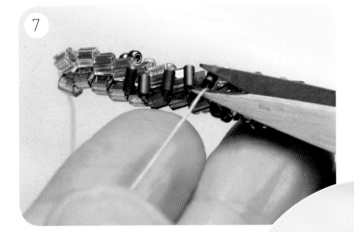

7 Pass the old thread back down through a few Delicas on the opposite side and secure with a half-hitch knot as before. Take the needle through a few more beads and then trim the end. Continue adding beads, joining on new threads as required, until the rope is about 1.5m (59in) long.

8 To make a tassel strand, using the tail thread, pick up four seed beads, a Delica, four seed beads, a bugle, four seed beads, a Delica and four seed beads. Pick up a cylinder bead and a seed bead, then pass the needle back up through the cylinder bead and the rest of the beads on the strand.

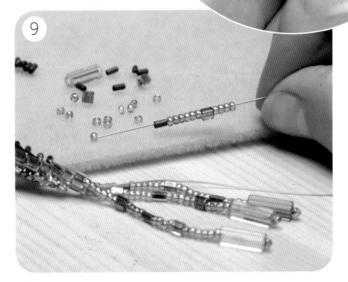

9 Take the needle through one Delica at the end of the bead rope and back out the other one ready to add another bead strand. Vary the number of seed beads picked up each time to create a range of strand lengths. Make about nine or ten strands on each end to create the tassels. Secure the thread ends with half-hitch knots and a drop of jewellery glue.

Chunky Loops Bracelet

YOU WILL NEED

⊙ 10g each of size 8 double Delica seed beads in cinnamon gold lustre and lined light blue ⊙ 5g of bugles in purple iris matt metal, 3mm ⊙ 5g each of size 11 seed beads in steel blue metallic, light sapphire grey lustre AB and s-l aqua ⊙ Multifilament thread, size D ⊙ 2 silver-plated shorteners, 10mm diameter ⊙ Beading needle ⊙ Basic tool kit (see pages 20–21)

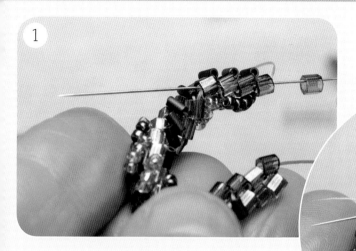

1 To make the rings for the bracelet, work a length of double-core bead rope with 20 cinnamon and 20 blue double Delicas in the same way as the Twist and Snake Necklace, Steps 1-4, pages 78-79. Keeping the twist, bring the tail round to the working end in a circle so that the Delica colours match. Take the thread through several cinnamon Delica beads.

You can tie the end rings together with ribbon for a different look.

2 Bring the thread back through the blue Delicas and then take the needle through a few beads on the other side. Fill in the diagonal lines of four seed beads and the bugles, keeping in sequence, by going backwards and forwards through the beads to finish off the rope circle. Sew in the ends securely, adding a drop of jewellery glue on the last knot, and trim the ends.

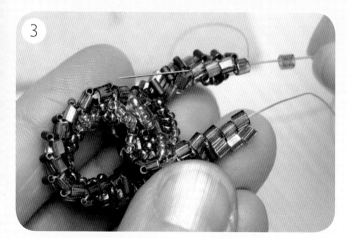

3 To make the bracelet, join each subsequent ring through a previous ring. Make enough rings to fit around your wrist (ten for a 15cm/6in circumference wrist measurement) and join the two ends with a shortener attached to each.

Untie the seed bead strings at one end and secure with bead stopper springs (see page 112). Remove the mesh from one scarf clip and tie the strings across one side. Loop half the wire through a resin leaf and take the ends through the mesh near the edge (see page 123). Attach one or two more leaves around the edge. Bring the wire out in the middle of the mesh and pick up a small pearl and a resin flower. Take the wire back through the flower and the mesh and pull taut. Continue adding flowers to cover the mesh, adding a few larger pearls and a few blue-green seed beads to fill any gaps. Check that the bead strings are the same length and tie the threads to the other mesh. Cover this mesh with a slightly different arrangement of flowers and leaves. Twist the tails of wire together and trim. Insert the meshes into the scarf clip backs and squeeze the metal lugs down to secure.

Flower Fancy

YOU WILL NEED

⊙ Seed bead strings in blue-green gloss, 6 50cm (20in) strings of size 6 ⊙ 5 resin leaves in blue-green, 15mm ⊙ 24 resin flowers in pastel shades, 8–15mm ⊙ Pearls in ivory, 24 3–4mm, 10 6mm ⊙ Silver-plated wire, 2m (2⅛yd) of 0.315mm (30swg) ⊙ 2 silver-plated scarf clips, 28mm ⊙ Basic tool kit (see pages 20–21)

MATINEE LENGTH (see page 25)

Arrange the beads in two rows, beginning with a coin-shaped ceramic bead, then a large resin bead. Begin the repeat pattern: clear flower, rust ceramic, brass washer, glazed ceramic, clear round, brass washer, brown diamond, cream faceted, clear flower, cracked glass nugget, brown bicone. Repeat the pattern four times on each side, then arrange an assortment of beads between the two ends to make a necklace at least 1m (39in) long. String on the silk cord. Thread each headpin with a round clear bead, a brown bicone and a cream faceted bead and make a plain loop at the end (see page 118). Thread one headpin dangle on one end of the silk cord. Pass the thread back through the ceramic coin bead, tie a half-hitch knot (see page 124) and then pass the thread through the resin bead. Trim the thread end. Repeat on the other end, making sure that the thread is taut before you trim the end.

Rustic Charm

YOU WILL NEED

⊙ 2 antiqued ceramic coin-shaped beads in rust, approx. 15mm ⊙ 11 antiqued ceramic mixed-shaped beads in rust, approx. 15mm ⊙ 2 ribbed resin beads in cream, 25 x 22mm ⊙ 22 clear plastic flower beads, 10mm ⊙ 22 brass washer beads, 6mm ⊙ 11 glazed ceramic beads in cream, 10mm ⊙ 13 clear plastic round beads, 8mm ⊙ 11 pressed glass diamond beads in brown, 14 x 12mm ⊙ 13 faceted beads in cream, 10mm ⊙ 11 cracked glass nuggets in red, 15 x 10mm ⊙ 12 pressed glass bicone beads in brown, 12 x 10mm ⊙ Natural silk bead cord with built-in needle, size 16 ⊙ 2 gold-plated headpins ⊙ Basic tool kit (see pages 20–21)

ROPE LENGTH (see page 25)

Make each of the cylinder beads into bead links with the wire (see page 118). Add a faceted bead either side of the Pandora beads and make these into bead links. Cut the chains into 5cm (2in) lengths. Attach two fine pieces of chain to a Pandora bead link and attach a cylinder bead link to the other ends. Attach a heavier chain length to the other side of the cylinder bead link. Make a headpin charm with the lariat tube (see page 118) and attach to the heavier chain length. This length of necklace must be able to fit through the lariat loop. Join on the remaining bead links and lengths of chain, adding a solid ring at intervals. Attach the lariat loop to this end using the jump ring (see page 120).

Chain Reaction

YOU WILL NEED

⊙ 9 ceramic cylinder beads in a silver finish, 10 x 6mm ⊙ 8 faceted beads each in matt pale blue and lime, 6mm ⊙ 8 silver-plated Pandora beads in lime/black/pale blue stripe, 13 x 9mm ⊙ Silver-plated oval solid rings, 2 x 1.5cm ⊙ Silver-plated wire, 0.6mm (24swg) ⊙ 4 different styles of silver-plated chain in mixed sizes, 25cm (10in) of each ⊙ Silver-plated decorative headpin ⊙ Silver-plated jump ring ⊙ Lariat loop and tube set ⊙ Basic tool kit (see pages 20–21)

ROPE LENGTH (see page 25)

Sautoir

Sautoir is a French word meaning 'long-chain necklace', and long they certainly are, since these fabulous items of jewellery can hang down as far as waist level. Sautoirs have been in and out of vogue throughout history, their simple elegance a welcome contrast to more opulent, ornate styles of necklace. Because of the length, it is essential to take the weight of beads into consideration when designing a sautoir and look for ways to keep the necklace as light as possible. Mixing lightweight plastic or hollow metal beads with glass or ceramic beads is effective or space the heavier beads with lengths of chain, ribbon, cord or strings of seed beads. To add the perfect finishing touch, create a matching tassel or add an attractive focal bead or pendant.

Linked in Time: assemble an interesting collection of antique gold chains to make this fabulous sautoir. Look for hollow metal beads, which are large but light and ideal for such a long necklace, then mix in a few ceramic beads and link together with the chain. Add a large focal bead to create a 'head' for the chain tassel.

Midnight and Moonshine: onyx and agate, both forms of the semi-precious mineral quartz, make stunning beads. Look for black agate beads that have a volcanic appearance and string them with shiny black onyx and hollow metal beads, adding an antique silver heart charm at the bottom instead of a tassel.

Lime and Raspberry Splash: gorgeous pearl beads in intense and contrasting colours are spaced with matching seed beads to make this arresting sautoir, which would look stunning against a plain, dark, fine wool sweater. Use two strands of a strong nylon thread for each string of seed beads for extra security.

Bead Creative

- Since these necklaces are so long, they are more comfortable to wear if you avoid placing large beads at the back of the neck.
- Using seed beads or short lengths of chain to space larger beads will reduce the weight of the necklace.
- Look for unusual large beads or charms to create a focal point at the bottom of the necklace.

Peacock Plume: a beautiful beaded tassel makes a stunning focal point for this exotic necklace, which has been cleverly created with herringbone stitch incorporating large filigree beads along its length. Herringbone is a quick bead-stitching technique, especially if you use long twisted bugles. The tassel can be untied from the necklace and attached to a key ring or alternatively used as a bag charm (see page 89).

Peacock Plume

YOU WILL NEED

⊙ 50g of 7mm twisted bugles in purple iris gloss ⊙ 10g of size 11 seed beads in sapphire purple lustre AB ⊙ 5g of size 6 seed beads in matt nickel ⊙ Metal filigree beads in grey, 1 25 x 15mm, 2 18 x 15mm and 4 15 x 10mm ⊙ 5g of 3mm bugles in nickel matt
⊙ 5g of size 11 Toho triangles in blue iris metallic iridescent matt ⊙ 2 glazed ceramic beads,

1 Make a length of ladder stitch using eight 7mm twisted bugles, following Steps 1 and 2 on page 122. Join the ends together in a ring by passing the needle through the first and last bugles again so that the tail and working thread come out at opposite sides.

2 To begin the herringbone stitch, * pick up two twisted bugles and pass the needle down through the next bugle on the base tube and up through the next one along. Repeat from * all the way around.

3 When working tubular herringbone stitch, you always 'step up' at the end of a round ready to begin the next round. To do this, simply pass the needle back through the next bugle on the base tube and the bugle above it.

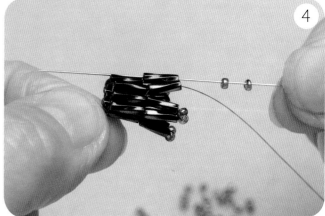

4 On the next round, add size 11 seed beads. Pick up two seed beads and take the needle back down through the next bugle. Go back up through the next bugle along ready to add the next two seed beads. Continue to the end of the round and step up through the next bugle and seed bead.

20 x 15mm ⊙ Braided beading thread in smoke grey, size D ⊙ Quilting thread in black or grey ⊙ Silver-plated wire, 0.6mm (24swg) ⊙ Organza ribbon in lilac, 15mm (⅝in) ⊙ Beading needle, size 10 ⊙ Basic tool kit (see pages 20–21)

MATINEE LENGTH
(see page 25)

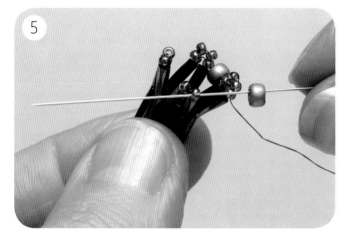

5 Add the size 6 seed beads between the pairs of seed beads on the next round. * Pick up two seed beads and pass the needle back down through the next seed bead. Pick up a size 6 seed bead and pass the needle back up through the next seed bead along. Repeat from * to the end of the round.

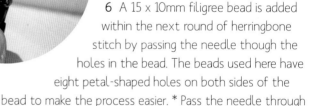

6 A 15 x 10mm filigree bead is added within the next round of herringbone stitch by passing the needle though the holes in the bead. The beads used here have eight petal-shaped holes on both sides of the bead to make the process easier. * Pass the needle through from one side of the filigree bead to the other, pick up two size 11 seed beads and pass the needle back through the next holes along, going back through the size 11 seed bead, the size 6 seed bead and the next size 11 seed bead. Repeat from * all the way around. There will be four pairs of seed beads on the top of the filigree bead. As in Step 5, add size 6 seed beads between the pairs of seed beads in the next round of herringbone stitch.

7 The rounds then continue with this pattern block: two rounds of twisted bugles, two rounds of size 11 seed beads, one round of nickel bugles, one round of triangles, one round of nickel bugles, two rounds of size 11 seed beads and two rounds of twisted bugles.

Felt beads would make an interesting alternative if you can't find filigree beads.

Peacock Plume

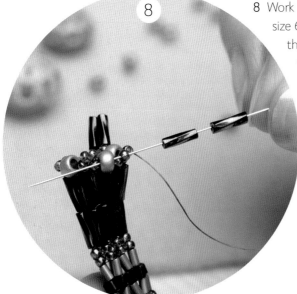

8 Work two rounds of size 11 seed beads, adding size 6 seed beads on the second round. Work the pattern block in Step 7 on page 87. Repeat from Step 4 on page 86 again, adding a medium-sized filigree bead this time. Repeat from Step 4 again, adding one of the small filigree beads.

9 Put this length of beadwork to one side and make another exactly the same. Join a thread to the bugle band at the end you started at and continue the pattern to finish one block, then work a further seven blocks without adding filigree beads, only size 6 seed beads.

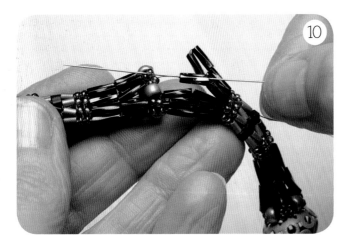

10 Continue the pattern until you have added the two rows of seed beads after the nickel bugles and join on the length of beadwork you put to one side by passing the needle backwards and forwards through the two rows of herringbone stitch. Sew in the end and secure with a half-hitch knot (see page 124). At the other end, complete three pattern blocks between the two small filigree beads, joining the ends to make a complete circle. Make a tassel (see opposite) and attach with ribbon to finish.

When adding the first lot of twisted bugles, pass the needle through the size 6 seed bead each time.

Tassel Charm

2 Tie the threads in an overhand knot near the top of the beads (see page 124). Loop a length of the silver-plated wire under the knot and wind around to secure. Trim the thread and pick up a ceramic bead, a large filigree bead and a ceramic bead.

1 To make the tassel, pick up a size 11 seed bead on a length of quilting thread. Pass both ends through a 11.5cm (4½in) big-eye needle. Pick up a size 6 seed bead, * two size 11 seed beads, two twisted bugles, two size 11 seed beads, a nickel bugle, a triangle and a nickel bugle. Repeat from * and then pull the threads through the beads. Make 15 bead strands in all.

3 Make a wrapped loop at the top to finish the tassel (see page 119) and trim the wire end neatly. Thread the tassel with ribbon. Tie around the sautoir or a bag handle (see right).

If the ceramic bead has a large hole, fill with smaller beads (size 6 seed beads should be ideal) or fill with polymer clay (see page 14).

Linked in Time

YOU WILL NEED

⊙ 6 bronze metal round and oval beads, 15–20mm ⊙ 4 bronze metal square, flat beads, 25mm ⊙ 5 glazed ceramic beads in cream, 15mm ⊙ Cut-glass crystal in brown, 25 x 35mm ⊙ 3 different styles of antique gold or bronze chains in mixed sizes, 30cm (12in) of each ⊙ 16 antique gold eyepins ⊙ Basic tool kit (see pages 20–21)

MATINEE LENGTH (see page 25)

Make each bead into a bead link, as follows. Thread the bead on to an eyepin, bend the end of the eyepin over at an angle and trim to 7mm (³⁄₈in), then use round-nosed pliers to form the tail into a loop (see page 118). To make the tassel, join the large crystal to a ceramic bead. Attach six short lengths of chain to the loop below the ceramic bead. Join each of the square beads to two other beads to make three groups of beads. Cut short lengths of chain, between 5cm (2in) and 10cm (4in), and join two different styles to the wire loop above the crystal. Add a single bead link to one side and a group to the other. Join the other bead links with chain in between, adding a plain length of chain to join the two ends that will sit at the back of the wearer's neck.

Midnight and Moonshine

YOU WILL NEED
⊙ 37 black onyx frosted beads, 4mm ⊙ 65 black onyx frosted beads, 6mm
⊙ 18 black agate beads, 10mm ⊙ 14 black agate beads, 14mm ⊙ 16
antique silver ribbed beads, 4 x 8mm ⊙ 15 antique silver beads, 8 x 13mm
⊙ Decorative metallic heart charm, 25 x 30mm ⊙ Bead thread, 2m (2⅛yd)
of 0.46mm (0.018in) ⊙ 64 silver-plated twisted wire jump rings, 6mm
⊙ Basic tool kit (see pages 20–21)

MATINEE LENGTH (see page 25)

Pick up 35
of the 4mm onyx beads
and drop them to the middle of the
bead thread. Each side of the necklace is the
same, so on both sides pick up a 6mm onyx bead,
jump ring, 10mm agate bead, jump ring, 6mm onyx
bead and an antique silver ribbed bead. Repeat again with a
large antique silver bead instead of the ribbed bead and then
repeat both sequences once more. Continue the sequence
using 14mm agate beads instead of 10mm, then finish with four
10mm agates in the sequence. Pick up a 4mm onyx bead on
the end of each string, then thread both strings through a
large antique silver bead, a 14mm agate bead and a 6mm
onyx bead. Thread on the heart charm, take the
threads back through several beads and secure
with half-hitch knots (see page 124). Take the
tails through several more beads and
trim the ends.

Lime and Raspberry Splash

YOU WILL NEED
⊙ 10g each of size 11 seed beads in topaz
raspberry lustre AB and transparent lime
⊙ Round pearls in purple, 2 15mm and 5 10mm
⊙ Round pearls in lime, 2 15mm and 4 10mm
⊙ Pearl-shaped beads, 2 in lime and 2 in
purple, 20 x 25mm ⊙ Faceted bead in purple,
12 x 25mm ⊙ Faceted bead in purple,
25 x 35mm ⊙ Seed bead in transparent lime,
size 6 ⊙ Nylon bead string in purple and lime,
size A ⊙ Bead spinner ⊙ Curved big-eye
needle ⊙ Basic tool kit (see pages 20–21)

MATINEE LENGTH (see page 25)

Cut two 1.3m (51in)
lengths of bead string in both colours.
Using a bead spinner and the curved big-eye
needle, string 30cm (12in) of the raspberry seed
beads on the purple bead string (see page 113). Use a
straight big-eye needle to pick up a large round purple pearl
on each side, then change to a curved big-eye needle and pick
up 4cm (1½in) of raspberry seed beads, then a small round purple
pearl. Adding 4cm (1½in) of seed beads between the pearls, pick up
the remaining beads in the order shown in the photo of the necklace.
Repeat with the lime thread and beads, taking the needle through
the large beads already strung. String the small lime pearls on the
green thread only and then pass the needle through the next
large bead. Take all four sets of threads through a small purple
pearl and the two faceted purple beads. Pick up the size 6
green seed bead and take the threads back through
the faceted beads, securing with two half-hitch
knots (see page 124) and a drop of
jewellery glue.

Knotted Necklace

Knotting is an elementary technique that usually keeps a low profile in necklace design, as it has a primarily utilitarian function, spacing pearls or other precious beads to avoid them rubbing or to prevent beads being lost if the necklace breaks. But here the knot is celebrated, making it a major feature in each design and as important, if not more so, than the beads themselves. The necklace opposite uses macramé, a traditional knotting technique, in a thoroughly modern way bringing together a fabulous yarn, pony beads and a huge donut pendant to make a stunning necklace. But don't stop there – traditional stringing materials such as waxed cotton and bead cord are now available in a huge range of pretty colours that look fabulous knotted between all sorts of beads.

Fruity Fun: this fresh, colourful necklace is ideal for wearing on a summer's day and would look equally good with a simple T-shirt or a pretty dress. The beads are knotted on to waxed cord and organza ribbon, which are tied to one side to create a focal point.

Wood Works: giant wood beads would have been rather dark and dull on their own in a necklace, but teamed with paler wood beads with a pretty painted design changes the look completely. The blue and brown colour scheme is echoed in the knotted waxed cord to add to the overall effect.

Candy Cords: this knotted necklace features a trompe l'oeil effect, as in reality it would be impossible to get so many threads through the beads! Extra threads are simply added after the beads have been strung. A carefully chosen mix of beads in candy colours with varying surface interest completes the look.

Bead Creative

- Try using different materials such as ribbon, yarn or tubular metal mesh to string the beads.
- If beads don't have a large enough hole for stringing thicker materials, make into a headpin charm (see page 118) and attach to the knot with a jump ring.
- Vary the knots, tying a reef (square) knot or a figure-of-eight knot (see page 124) instead of the usual overhand knot between the beads.

Macramé Magic: macramé is enjoying a revival, and no wonder, as there are so many fabulous decorative yarns to work with. This double-knitting weight yarn is ideal, picking up the green and purple of the beads while adding a little sparkle with the fine lurex thread. The design is worked in alternating square knot (see page 123), and finished professionally with antique gold end bars. If you don't have much time, you can make a funky key charm instead (see page 97).

Macramé Magic

YOU WILL NEED

⊙ Donut bead in green, 5.75cm (2¼in) ⊙ 36 pony beads in purple, 6 x 8mm ⊙ 2 antique gold end bars ⊙ Multicoloured knitting yarn in green, gold and purple with lurex thread, 12m (13¼yd) of double-knitting thickness ⊙ Antique gold lobster claw necklace fastening ⊙ Low-tack tape ⊙ Stick-on note ⊙ Basic tool kit (see pages 20–21)

1 Cut eight 1.5m (59in) lengths of the yarn and separate into four pairs. Fold each pair in half, push the folded end through the hole in the donut and then pass the tails through the loop.

2 Pull the thread tails through until the loops are tight, then separate two sets to each side of the donut. Secure the donut to the work surface with low-tack tape ready to work one side of the macramé necklace.

3 To begin the square knot on the first four strands of yarn, take the left strand under the two strands in the middle and over the right-hand strand.

4

5

5 Add a pony bead
to the centre two
strands of yarn.
If you twist the
strands together
for a short length
and then fold in
half, you should
be able to push the
tight twist through
the bead.

4 Take the right strand over the middle
strands and through the loop formed on
the left-hand side. Pull the strands through
to make a half knot (see the diagrams on
page 123).

6

Always work the knots in the same way
on the left and the opposite way on the
right for a balanced effect.

6 After adding the bead, work a complete square knot (see
the diagrams on page 123). Work a half knot on the other set
of strands and add a bead.

Macramé Magic

7 Work a square knot after the bead again and then pull the outside strands through to tighten the knot. To work a square knot in the centre, move the outer two strands on each side out a little, leaving four strands in the middle. Tie a square knot over the centre two strands.

8 Sort the strands out again into two bundles of four. Tie a square knot on each side. Add a pony bead to each pair of middle strands and work a square knot underneath each bead. Repeat Steps 7 and 8 until you have added 18 beads, finishing with a centre square knot, then two more square knots.

For best results, begin with the right thread first on the left-hand set of strands and the left thread first on the right-hand set.

9 Work the other side of the necklace in the same way. Endeavour to keep the same tension so that each side is the same length. Cut a 1cm (½in) gummed strip of stick-on note and stick behind the strands. Trim the thread ends to leave a 3mm (⅛in) strip of paper.

10 Apply a little jewellery glue over the strands and then tuck the trimmed end into the end bar fastening. Close the end bar with flat-nosed pliers, making sure that the paper and thread ends are tucked securely inside. Repeat to finish the other side, then attach a lobster claw necklace fastening to finish.

Textural Key Charm

YOU WILL NEED

⊙ Key ring finding ⊙ Multicoloured yarn in green, gold and purple with lurex thread, 2.5m (2¾yd) of double-knitting thickness ⊙ 12 pony beads in purple, 9 x 7mm ⊙ Cube bead in purple, 4.5 x 4cm ⊙ Low-tack tape ⊙ Needle and sewing thread ⊙ Basic tool kit (see pages 20–21)

Secure the key ring to the work surface with low-tack tape once you have added the yarn so that you can tie the macramé knots easily.

Cut four 1.25m (49in) lengths of yarn and fold each in half. Attach each length to the key ring with a lark's head knot (see page 124). * Work a square knot with the centre four threads, then a square knot on each of the four outer threads (see Steps 3-4, pages 94-95). Thread a pony bead on to the two middle threads of these square knots and then work another square knot under each bead. Repeat from *. Work alternate centre square knots and outer square knots until you have added 8 pony beads and completed five centre square knots. Thread on the cube bead. Continuing as you did at the start, add four pony beads with the next two sets of outer square knots and then work two centre square knots to finish. Trim the thread ends to 1cm (½in). Fold the macramé up towards the key ring, tuck the thread ends under and sew the macramé in place with a needle and strong thread.

Fruity Fun

YOU WILL NEED

⊙ Painted heart bead in deep pink, 30mm ⊙ 25 painted wood beads in white spotted raspberry, red, pink and orange, 12 x 15mm ⊙ Wood pony beads in raspberry, orange and pink, 14 8 x 10mm and 8 6 x 8mm ⊙ Waxed cotton cord in orange, pink and raspberry, 2m (2⅛yd) of each ⊙ Organza ribbon in pink, 2m (2⅛yd) of 15mm (⅝in) ⊙ 2 spring cord ends ⊙ Hook necklace fastening ⊙ Basic tool kit (see pages 20–21)

1 Cut the cords and ribbon in half. Make two bundles the same and tie together with a reef (square) knot (see page 124), leaving 8-10cm (3-4in) tails. Feed the long cords on one side through the large heart-shaped bead and use a big-eye needle to thread the ribbon through. Tie an overhand knot after the bead. Guide it down with a tapestry needle and pull tight (see page 116).

MATINEE LENGTH
(see page 25)

2 Pick up a spotted raspberry and spotted red bead on orange and pink cords. Thread the remaining cord and ribbon through a large raspberry pony bead and tie an overhand knot with all the cords and ribbon. Repeat using spotted pink and orange beads with a small raspberry pony bead.

If you have to untie waxed cord because you make a mistake, refresh by ironing to restore the stiffness.

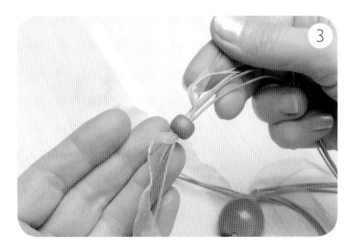

3 After the next knot, thread the cords and ribbon through a large pale pink pony bead and tie another overhand knot. * Add two spotted beads singly, knotting after each one, then another pony bead. Repeat from * to finish that side. On the opposite side, add two sets of double beads and three sets of single beads in a mix of colours.

4 Add one or two pony beads to each of the dangling cords and the ribbons coming from the reef knot. Tie them together in pairs. Trim the ends neatly. Check the length of the necklace so that the large heart bead sits as a 'station' at one side. Trim the necklace ends to the correct length and attach spring ends (see page 114). Attach a hook fastening.

Wood Works

YOU WILL NEED

⊙ 5 dark wood oval beads, approx. 50 x 32mm ⊙ 4 dark wood round ribbed beads, 24mm ⊙ 8 pale blue beads, 20mm ⊙ 5 dark blue beads, 20mm ⊙ 4 dark blue beads, 10mm ⊙ 8 painted wood beads, 30 x 15mm ⊙ Waxed cotton cord in pale blue and brown, 2m (2⅛yd) of 1mm each ⊙ Tapestry needle ⊙ Basic tool kit (see pages 20–21)

MATINEE LENGTH (see page 25)

Arrange the beads on a beading mat so that you have a dark wood bead with two or three coloured or painted wood beads in between. Holding both cords together, tie an overhand knot about 15cm (6in) from one end (see page 124). Thread a large dark wood bead on the long ends and drop it down to the knot. Tie a second overhand knot on the other side of the bead, using a tapestry needle to guide the knot to the right position (see page 116). Continue picking up beads in the order you have chosen, tying a knot after each one, until the necklace is about 90cm (35in) long. Untie the knot after the first large bead and take it off again. Thread just the brown cord through. Thread the other end of the brown cord through in the opposite direction. Tie an overhand knot both sides of the large bead, keeping the cord taut. Use jewellery glue to secure the knot and then trim the ends.

Candy Cords

YOU WILL NEED

⊙ 11 pressed glass mixed cylinder and shaped beads in burgundy, 12 x 9mm ⊙ Ceramic cylinder beads in a silver finish, 9 12 x 9mm and 9 6 x 4mm ⊙ 6 dimpled cylinder beads in pastel shades, 12 x 15mm ⊙ 6 glass pearl beads in vanilla, 14mm ⊙ Crocheted beads in pink, 1 22mm and 2 15mm ⊙ 2 silver-plated bell end cones, 15 x 6mm ⊙ Superlon bead cord in pale lemon, size 18 ⊙ Silver-plated wire, 0.6mm (24swg) ⊙ Necklace fastening ⊙ Tapestry needle ⊙ Basic tool kit (see pages 20–21)

MATINEE LENGTH (see page 25)

Tie an overhand knot 15cm (6in) from one end of four 60cm (23½in) lengths of bead cord (see page 124). Thread on a glass bead and tie another overhand knot, using a tapestry needle to guide the knot into the right position (see page 116). * Pick up a small silver cylinder, a dimpled bead and a larger silver cylinder. Tie an overhand knot. Repeat with a selection of beads until there are 24 in all. Make a shorter necklace length with four more lengths of bead cord and the remaining 20 beads. Check that the two strands hang well together and then tie overhand knots after the last bead on each length. Tie two threads from each bundle together at both ends. Cut two lots of eight 40cm (16in) lengths of bead cord. Tuck one bundle under the tied thread and tie an overhand knot with all the threads. Repeat with the other end. Tie another overhand knot at the end of each thread bundle. Wrap with silver-plated wire, leaving a tail, and attach bell end cones (see page 115). Form the tail into a plain or wrapped loop with round-nosed pliers and attach a necklace fastening.

Floating Necklace

These exquisite necklaces are designed to give the illusion that the beads are floating around your neck. The stringing material – illusion cord, a clear monofilament thread or bead stringing wire – is of secondary importance and almost seems non-existent. The beads are usually spaced out along the stringing material, and this is the challenge of these necklaces, as you endeavour to secure the beads in as neat a way as possible. Crimps, either donut- or tubular-shaped, are ideal for spacing beads on bead stringing wire. For the more delicate illusion cord, simply loop the cord through small beads and pull tight. This creates a kink that is sufficient to support the bead; for larger beads you can incorporate a knot (see page 124) or add a drop of jewellery glue.

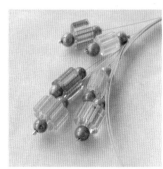

Funky Lime: the natural spring of bead stringing wire has been harnessed to create this unusual modern design. One set of bead strings has the zingy, citrus-coloured beads attached, while the ends of the other set are secured inside a single bead with a large crimp.

Crystal Falls: two high-quality faceted beads – firepolish and Swarovski crystals – are combined to make this sumptuous, light-catching necklace. Each string features a different-coloured firepolish bead. The crystals can be secured with a drop of jewellery glue or left loose to slide up and down.

Pearl Illusion: a gorgeous selection of pearls and unusual-shaped beads make this floating necklace extra special. The classic combination of turquoise, white and gold beads are secured on the illusion cord in a relatively random way yet give a balanced effect overall.

Bead Creative

○ If you want the stringing material to 'disappear', choose one of the finer thicknesses of illusion cord or bead stringing wire.
○ Look out for coloured bead stringing wire and coordinate the colour with your beads.
○ Try making hidden joins with bead stringing wire by securing the ends inside a large bead.

Silver Sensation: the classic illusion necklace, often made ➤ *with tiny pearls, is given a contemporary makeover with these sensational silver beads. The beads may be large, but they are hollow and extremely light so therefore can be strung on very fine illusion cord, appearing to float in mid-air. Tiny silver-lined seed beads are added for extra sparkle. Use the same bead ingredients and techniques to make a pair of glamorous earrings to match (see page 107).*

Silver Sensation

YOU WILL NEED

⊙ Silver-plated stardust round beads, 20 8mm, 30 6mm and 75 4mm
⊙ 5g of size 8 silver-lined twisted hex beads ⊙ 5g of size 6 clear, silver-lined seed beads ⊙ Illusion cord, 0.3mm (0.012in) ⊙ 2 silver-plated E-Z crimp

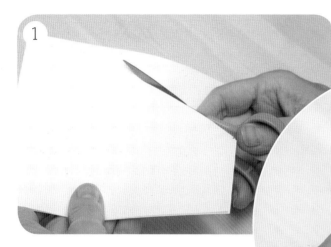

1 To make a template for the necklace, cut a strip of paper 30 x 12cm (12 x 4¾in) and fold in half crossways. Measure down 5cm (2in) at the open ends and cut a gentle diagonal curve down to the bottom of the fold side. Open out the template and pin to a large beading mat.

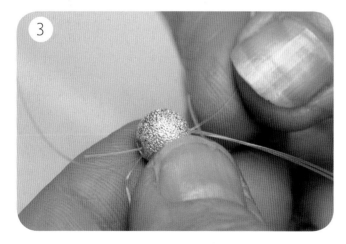

2 Cut a 60cm (23½in) length of illusion cord and several 40cm (16in) pieces. Lay one of the short pieces in the middle of the long length and tie together with an overhand knot so that the knot is in the middle of both lengths (see page 124).

3 Pick up an 8mm stardust bead and drop it down over the knot. Pass one long tail back through the bead. Take the tail between the bead and the illusion cord and then through the loop just formed. Pull up to form a half-hitch knot beside the bead (see Illusion Bead Knot, page 124).

4 Pull the pair of cords at the opposite side of the bead to the knot and tug until the knot disappears inside the bead, leaving two threads out each side. Add a drop of instant glue into the hole of the bead at one side to secure.

ends or clamshell calottes ☉ Necklace fastening ☉ Cyanoacrylate instant glue
☉ Tapestry needle ☉ Basic tool kit (see pages 20–21)

CHOKER LENGTH
(see page 25)

5 Lay the long strand with small stop beads on each side across the top of the template and pin in place. Add beads to the two shorter strands.

To prevent the illusion cord becoming kinked, secure it with bead stopper springs at each and, rather than wrapping around the pins.

6 To secure the size 8 hex beads or smaller, simply secure with a drop of instant glue. Pick up a hex bead on one strand, add a drop of instant glue where you want the bead to lie and then use a tapestry needle to slide the bead over the drop of glue. Leave for a few moments until the glue sets.

7 To secure the size 6 beads or small round stardust beads, loop the illusion cord back through the bead: drop the bead down the cord and pass the end back through the bead. Hold the loop taut at one end and add a drop of instant glue to the other. Hold for a few moments until the glue sets.

Silver Sensation

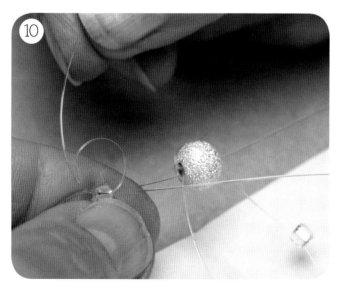

8 Larger beads, having big holes, are more difficult to simply glue, so use an illusion bead knot to secure, as in Step 3, page 104. Pass the illusion cord back through the bead, then take the tail between the bead and the cord and back through the loop just formed. Pull to form a half-hitch knot beside the bead. Pull the cord at the other end of the bead to pull the knot inside the bead.

9 Continue adding beads on both strands, alternating between small and larger beads, until you are near the bottom of the template. Add a hex or one of the other small beads and secure with a drop of instant glue. Trim the tail close to the bead once it has dried.

Great care should be taken when working with instant glue, as it can stick to skin very quickly.

10 Remove the bead stopper spring at one side of the necklace and then add a seed bead. Secure a second short strand as in Step 2, page 104, about 1cm (½in) from the previous bead and add another medium or large bead over the top. Pass the tail through the bead and again secure with a loop and half-hitch knot.

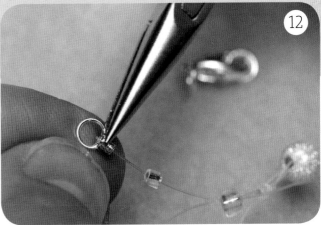

11 Continue adding illusion cord strands and beads along the main necklace strand, shaping the strand lengths to fit the template. To add more weight and beads to the necklace, you can go back along the main strand tying on more cord strands using a reef (square) knot (see page 124).

12 Once the necklace has enough beaded strands along its length, check the length and add the E-Z crimp ends as shown here to both ends or attach silver-plated clamshell calottes (see page 115). Attach a necklace fastening.

Stardust Sparkle Earrings

YOU WILL NEED

⊙ 16 clear, silver-lined seed beads, size 6 ⊙ Silver-plated stardust round beads, 4 8mm, 10 6mm and 9 4mm ⊙ 50 silver-lined twisted hex beads, size 8 ⊙ Illusion cord, 0.3mm (0.012in) ⊙ 2 silver-plated earring findings ⊙ Cyanoacrylate instant glue ⊙ Basic tool kit (see pages 20–21)

The earrings can be made longer or shorter to suit your hairstyle or preference.

To make one earring, cut five 35cm (13¾in) lengths of illusion cord and insert into the loop of the earring finding. Fold the cord in half, thread on a seed bead and apply a drop of instant glue. Add an 8mm stardust bead and secure with a loop and half-hitch knot (see Step 3, page 104). Add beads to each strand in the same way as for the necklace (see pages 105-107). Vary the lengths of the strands, with the longest about 10cm (4in). Trim the tails after the last bead on each strand. Make a second earring to match by copying each strand in turn from the first earring.

Funky Lime

YOU WILL NEED

⊙ Selection of 7 plastic beads in lime and orange, approx. 1–1.2cm ⊙ Miracle beads, 6 in lime and 6 in orange, 6mm ⊙ Bead stringing wire in lime, 3.5m (4yd) ⊙ 4 tubular crimps, size 3 ⊙ 12 donut crimps, size 0 ⊙ 2 silver-plated thong ends ⊙ 2 silver-plated jump rings ⊙ Necklace fastening ⊙ Basic tool kit (see pages 20–21)

CHOKER LENGTH
(see page 25)

1 Cut six 24cm (9½in) lengths and six 30cm (12in) lengths of the bead stringing wire. Secure one end of each bundle with a tubular crimp (see page 116). Insert the crimped end into a thong end and close each side with flat-nosed pliers (see page 114). Attach the necklace fastening with jump rings (see page 120).

2 Feed a large triangular-shaped plastic bead followed by two tubular crimps on to the long strand and position the crimps about 18cm (7in) from the thong end. Tuck the other strand ends through the crimps from the opposite direction. Secure the crimps with a pair of crimping pliers (see page 116). Glue the bead over the top of the crimps.

Mock up the necklace to check the length and position of the single large, triangular-shaped bead before crimping in place.

3 Pick up a size 1 crimp, and using crimping pliers, secure about 2.5cm (1in) from the large plastic bead. Add a miracle bead, a plastic bead, another miracle bead and a crimp. Secure the crimp with pliers. Repeat on each of the six strands, securing the first crimp down a further 1cm (½in) each time. Trim the tails of the wires.

Crystal Falls

YOU WILL NEED

⊙ Firepolish faceted beads, 7 each in purple, rose and light pink, 12mm
⊙ Swarovski crystals, 8 each in purple, rose and light pink, 4mm ⊙ Bead stringing wire in three shades of pink, 50cm (20in) of each ⊙ Approx. 42 antique copper crimps ⊙ 2 antique copper clamshell calottes ⊙ Antique copper necklace fastening ⊙ Cyanoacrylate instant glue ⊙ Basic tool kit (see pages 20–21)

MATINEE LENGTH (see page 25)

Add one
colour of bead to each
wire. Using flat-nosed pliers, secure
a crimp 6cm (2½in) from the end of one
wire. * Pick up a firepolish bead and secure with
another crimp. Pick up a crystal. Secure another crimp
4cm (1½in) away from the previous crimp, leaving the
crystal loose in between. Repeat from * until you have
seven of each bead on the wire. Attach a bead stopper spring
(see page 112). Make two more strands using the other beads,
beginning 8cm (3in) down on one and 10cm (4in) down on
the other, but spacing beads as before. Add a crystal to the
beginning of each wire and arrange so that the beads hang
attractively. Trim the ends to the same level. Attach a
clamshell calotte with crimps (see page 115) and then
a necklace fastening. Finally, secure each of the
crystals centrally between the larger
beads using a drop of instant glue.

Pearl Illusion

YOU WILL NEED

⊙ 25 round pearls in ivory, 3mm ⊙ 20 round pearls in ivory, 7mm ⊙ Shaped beads in turquoise, 3–10mm, 20 3mm round, 15 8mm flat disc and 12 10mm orange segment ⊙ Approx. 12 metal-effect round beads in a gold finish ⊙ Approx. 12 pressed glass beads in mottled green, 3 x 8mm ⊙ Clear illusion cord, 0.3mm (0.012in) ⊙ Tubular crimp necklace fastening ⊙ Cyanoacrylate instant glue ⊙ Basic tool kit (see pages 20–21)

MATINEE LENGTH (see page 25)

Cut ten 56cm (22in) lengths of the cord. Secure one set of ends in a bead stopper spring (see page 112). Pick up a small bead on the first length and drop it down to 8cm (3in) from the spring. Pass the cord back through the small bead and pull taut. Pick up a different small bead and secure in the same way 2-2.5cm (¾-1in) from the first. Continue adding beads in the same way or with a drop of instant glue, or use the illusion bead knot, page 124. Stop when you are 36cm (14in) from the first bead. Repeat with the other cords, changing the bead positions slightly so that they don't lie together. Trim the cord ends to length, allowing for the fastening. Insert one set of cords into one end. Squeeze flat with flat-nosed pliers. Repeat at the other end.

Jewellery Techniques

Each of the main designs in the book has precise instructions and accompanying photographs for making the necklaces, but the following pages demonstrate the core jewellery-making techniques involved in detail. There are also references to these techniques in the text-only instructions for the additional designs in each chapter, to allow you to create them as easily as possible. Even if you are an experienced beader, looking at these techniques will help to refresh your memory or to learn a new way of doing things.

Making a continuous loop

Necklaces over 61cm (24in) don't need a fastening, so select from the following methods to join the ends according to whichever type of stringing material you are using.

Elastic thread
Tie the ends of the thread together, working two reef (square) knots (see page 124) one after the other, and hide the knot inside one of the beads with a large hole.

Alternatively, feed the opposite ends through a crimp and squeeze to secure. Two crimps spaced a few beads apart is even more secure.

Working with cords and threads

Monofilament, bead stringing wire, waxed cotton, rattail (satin cord) and leather thong are just some of the materials used to string beads for jewellery (see pages 15–17). Each material has different properties and so there are several ways to finish the ends, secure beads and attach fastenings, depending on which you are using.

Bead stoppers

When working some necklace designs, it is essential to stop the beads falling off the end of the thread or bead stringing wire. Bead stopper springs are a great little tool for this purpose, or use a stop bead instead.

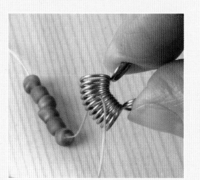

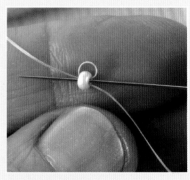

Using a bead stopper spring
Squeeze the levers on the bread spring and slot the thread or wire between the coils. You can move the spring up and down the thread as required.

Using a stop bead
Pick up a bead on the thread or wire and hold the bead about 10cm (4in) from the end. Take the needle back through the bead two or three times to secure.

Bead thread or cord

Tie the ends with a reef (square) knot (see page 124) and hide the knot in a bead with a larger hole, or use the following more secure technique:

1 Before you begin, make sure you can pass a double length of thread through the bead holes. String the beads, leaving 10cm (4in) at each end. Pass one end of the thread through five or six beads.

2 Using the tail thread, work a half-hitch knot (see page 124) over the main thread. Pass the end through another two beads and knot again. Secure each knot with a drop of jewellery glue. Repeat with the other tail, working in the opposite direction. Pass the ends through a few more beads and trim the ends neatly.

Bead stringing wire

As this stringing material can't be knotted, thread a crimp between two beads and add another crimp a few beads along. Thread the wire from the other end through both crimps. Pull the wire taut and secure the crimps with flat-nosed or crimping pliers (see page 116).

Crimping pliers come in several sizes, so be sure to use the correct size for your crimps.

Using a bead spinner

It takes a little practice to become proficient, but this tool, used in conjunction with a curved big-eye needle (see page 22), will enable you to string beads surprisingly quickly. Thread the needle. Pour beads into the spinner. Turn the handle slowly to get the beads spinning (they need not be moving quickly). Lower the threaded needle into the beads so that it is fairly horizontal and the beads should whiz up the needle.

Adding fastenings

Depending on the stringing material you are using, choose one of these techniques to attach the fastening.

Spring ends

Feed the ends of the cord right through the spiral crimp and trim the end. Move the spiral crimp slightly to hide the raw edges and squeeze only the bottom end ring to secure.

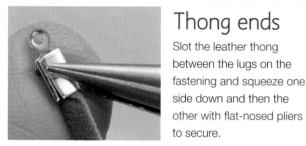

Thong ends

Slot the leather thong between the lugs on the fastening and squeeze one side down and then the other with flat-nosed pliers to secure.

Decorative crimp fastenings

These have a crimp incorporated into the design, and are ideal for finishing bead stringing wire or fine waxed cord. Insert the end of the wire into the fastening and squeeze the crimp ring with snipe-nosed or crimping pliers to secure.

Attaching fastenings with a crimp

Use this secure method to create a loop in bead stringing wire or monofilament thread so that you can attach a jump ring or fastening.

1 Thread the crimp on to the wire, pick up a jump ring or fastening and feed the tail back through the crimp to create a loop. Compress the crimp (see page 116) so that it sits 1–2mm ($\frac{1}{16}$–$\frac{1}{10}$ in) from the ring or fastening.

2 Continue stringing beads. At the other end, pick up a crimp and the jump ring or fastening. Feed the tail back through the crimp and a few beads. Compress the crimp as before and trim the tail between the beads.

Adding a knot cover

Calottes or clamshell calottes are used to cover the raw ends of thread, wire, cord or fine ribbon when stringing beads (see page 18). Calottes have a hole in the side and clamshell calottes have a hole in the hinge.

Using a knot

Feed the open calotte on to the thread or cord and tie a figure-of-eight or overhand knot (see page 124). Trim the end close to the knot. Bring the calotte down so that it covers the knot. Close the calotte with flat-nosed pliers.

Using a crimp

Bead stringing wires or other coated wires that cannot be knotted easily can be secured inside the calotte with a crimp.

Thread the wire through the clamshell calotte, pick up a crimp and squeeze to flatten it. Close the clamshell with flat-nosed pliers.

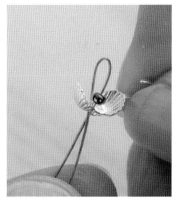

1 Alternatively, pick up a clamshell calotte and a seed bead. Feed the end back through the clamshell.

2 Take the wire through the next few beads and then pull the wire taut. Squeeze the crimp and trim the end. Close the clamshell with flat-nosed pliers.

Using end cones

These decorative findings are used to cover large knots at the end of necklaces or bracelets. They are particularly useful for multi-strand necklaces or for thick yarn or ribbon. Pick a style and size of end cone that will completely hide any knots or raw ends but fit snugly around the beads.

Bead stringing wire

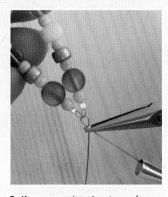

1 Finish multi-strand necklaces by making a loop on the end of each strand with a crimp. Attach the loops to an eyepin and feed the end through the end cone.

2 If you are planning to go from a multi-strand to a single-strand, make a crimp loop on a length of bead stringing wire and thread through the multi-strands.

Cord or ribbon

1 Tie a large overhand knot at the end of the cord or ribbon (see page 124). Wrap craft wire around the knot, leaving a tail at the top. Apply a few drops of jewellery glue over the knot before adding the end cone.

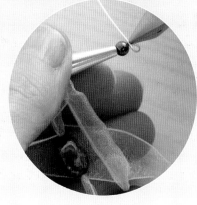

2 If necessary, add a small bead to reduce the hole size of the end cone. Use round-nosed pliers to make a plain or wrapped loop on the end of the wire (see pages 118–119), then attach a clasp.

Spacing beads

Beads can be spaced along a thread or wire in lots of different ways. The method you choose depends on the style of necklace and the stringing material.

Spacing beads with crimps

Bead stringing wires such as tigertail, Softflex and other coated wires can't be knotted and so the beads are spaced using crimps, which are available in a range of sizes. You can use flat-nosed pliers to secure the crimps or special crimping pliers for a more professional finish.

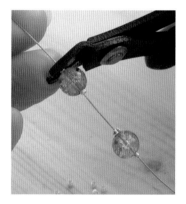

Secure a crimp on the wire. * Add a bead and a second crimp. Hold the wire up so that they drop down against the secured crimp. Squeeze the second crimp in position. Pick up another crimp and secure the desired distance from the first bead. Repeat from * until all the beads are added.

Using flat-nosed pliers

Squeeze the crimp with flat-nosed pliers until it is flat. The edges can be sharp, but as the crimp remains quite wide, this is often the best technique for beads with large holes.

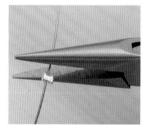

Using crimping pliers

Squeeze the crimp in the oval with the dip to make it curl. Move the crimp to the other oval and compress it into a rounded shape. This is the neatest technique for crimps that are used as a decorative feature in a necklace design.

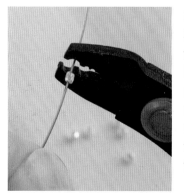

Spacing beads with knots

Bead strings are usually knotted to prevent the beads from rubbing together and also to stop all the beads falling off if the thread breaks. The traditional method is to use overhand knots, or try the quick and easy reef (square) knot technique opposite for a more casual necklace. Whichever method you choose, remember to allow an additional 3mm (⅛in) for each knot on finer threads and more for thicker threads.

Using overhand knots

This method is often used for stringing pearls. Add fastenings using a calotte or clamshell calotte (see pages 114–115).

1 Tie an overhand knot after the calotte or clamshell calotte by looping the tail over and under the main thread (see page 124). Pick up the first bead and then tie another loose overhand knot.

2 Slip a tapestry needle into the loop, then manoeuvre the knot along the cord until it is sitting next to the bead. Remove the needle as the knot tightens.

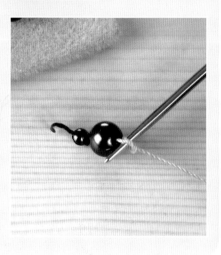

Using reef (square) knots

This is an easier technique to work, but the knots aren't quite as neat. It is ideal for necklaces with chunky beads.

1 Attach a fastening so that there is a double thread and tie a reef knot (see page 124). Use a big-eye needle (see page 21) to take both threads through the first bead.

2 Tie a reef knot on the other side of the bead. Pick up another bead using the big-eye needle and tie another reef knot. Repeat as required.

Working with wire

Wire used for jewellery making ranges from base metal brass or copper to sterling silver. The most popular wires are silver- or gold-plated, but coloured enamelled wires give a coordinated look to a necklace design. Wires are measured by the diameter of the wire in millimetres (mm) or in standard wire gauge (swg), and both measurements are given in the project 'You will need' lists. A good standard size that holds its shape in a bead link is 0.6mm (24swg). The higher the swg, the thinner the wire, so 36swg is a very fine 0.2mm and 18swg a chunky 1.2mm.

Cutting wire

You can always use strong craft scissors to cut finer wires, but it is better to invest in a pair of good-quality wire cutters, available from most beading shops (see page 20).

Wire cutters have a flat side and an angled side. Cut with the flat side towards the work to get a straight cut on the end of the wire. When cutting a wire that crosses over another wire, use the very tips of the blades to get as close as possible to the crossover point.

Twisting wire

You can use this technique to create texture, add body to the wire and make coiling and bending much smoother, as the wire is less likely to kink.

1 Use a bead to give you leverage for twisting the wire. Hold the bead between your finger and thumb and roll it round and round until the wire is evenly twisted along its length.

2 A cord maker or hand drill is ideal for twisting lengths of wire. Loop the wire over the hook, secure the ends in a vice and turn the handle to twist. Take care when releasing the wire, as it can spring up.

Bending wire

You need to apply firm pressure to get wire to bend where you want it to. Avoid pliers with a serrated surface, which will damage the wire.

Hold the wire firmly with flat-nosed pliers so that the edge of the jaw is exactly where you want the wire to bend. Rotate the pliers to create the particular angle. To create a right angle, hold the tail of the wire and push up against the jaws of the pliers with your thumb.

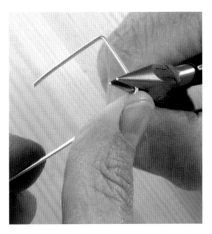

Jewellery Techniques

Making a bead link

Bead links have a loop at each end of the wire with one or more beads in the middle. This technique is easy to learn and ideal for beginners, but you can also use the headpin plain loop method shown right. If you use an eyepin to make the link, begin at Step 2 or use the plain loop method on the right.

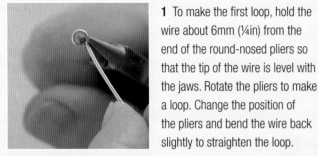

1 To make the first loop, hold the wire about 6mm (¼in) from the end of the round-nosed pliers so that the tip of the wire is level with the jaws. Rotate the pliers to make a loop. Change the position of the pliers and bend the wire back slightly to straighten the loop.

2 Feed the beads you require on to the end of the wire. Hold the wire in the jaws of the round-nosed pliers about 1mm (¹⁄₁₆in) from the beads. Wind the wire around the pliers to make a loop.

3 Cut the wire where it crosses using the very tip of the wire cutters (see page 117). Hold the ring with flat-nosed pliers and bend back to straighten.

Joining a link to a bead dangle

Use flat-nosed pliers to open one of the loops by pushing the cut end back, attach the other section and then close by reversing the action.

Using headpins and eyepins

Resembling large dressmaker's pins, headpins are used to make bead dangles or charms that can be hung from bracelets and necklaces or attached to bead links to make earrings. Eyepins are similar but have a large loop at one end.

Plain loop

This is an easier way to make a loop in headpins and eyepins, as they are made with a harder wire than normal jewellery wire. If the bead slides over the headpin, add a smaller bead such as a seed bead first.

1 Trim the wire to 7mm–1cm (⅜–½in) above the top bead. The distance will depend on the thickness of the wire and the size of the loop required. Make a right-angled bend close to the bead.

2 Hold the tip of the wire with round-nosed pliers and rotate the pliers to bend the wire partway around the tip. Reposition the pliers and continue rotating the pliers until the tip touches the wire and the loop is in the centre.

Wrapped loop

This is stronger than the plain loop and ideal for beads with slightly larger holes.

1 You will need at least 3cm (1¼in) of wire above the last bead. Hold the wire 1–2mm (¹⁄₁₆in) above the bead with snipe-nosed pliers and bend the wire at a right angle.

2 Hold the wire close to the bend with round-nosed pliers and wrap the tail all the way around to form a loop. Hold the loop firmly in round- or flat-nosed pliers and wind the wire tail around the stem, covering the gap between the loop and the bead. Trim the tail.

If the headpin pulls through the bottom bead, add a bead with a smaller hole first and then the larger bead.

Using filigree caps

These delicate metal caps are available in several sizes to suit different beads and look especially good with pearls. They give a piece of jewellery a more ornate and slightly antique look.

Select the correct size to fit the beads you are using. Add the filigree cap at one or both ends of the bead and then continue adding other beads.

Attaching earring wires

Earring wires have a split loop at the bottom that can be opened and closed in a similar way to jump rings (see page 120).

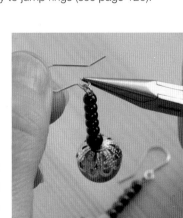

Hold the earring wire in one hand and the loop with flat-nosed pliers. Bring the pliers towards you to open. Attach the earring and reverse the action to close the loop.

Jump rings

One of the most versatile jewellery findings, jump rings are usually round and sometimes oval. They should never be pulled apart to open, as the shape will be distorted.

Opening and closing

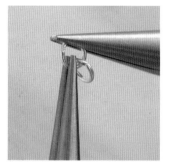

Hold the jump ring with two pairs of pliers, ideally both flat-nosed pliers, or use round-nosed with a pair of flat-nosed pliers. To open the ring, bring one pair of pliers towards you. Attach another ring, chain or jewellery finding. Reverse the action to close.

Making jump rings

1 Choose a rod of the required diameter – knitting needles are ideal. Hold the end of the wire at one end and wrap tightly around the rod.

2 Slide the closely wound spring off the needle. Use wire cutters to cut each jump ring in turn. Flip the wire cutters over to trim the end each time with the flat edge of the cutters before cutting the next ring.

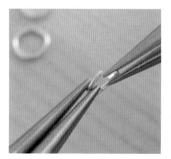

3 To tension the jump rings so that they stay closed, push the ends slightly so that they overlap on one side and then the other. Pull back and the ends will spring together.

Making chain with jump rings

This is an easy technique, and to speed up the process, you can join rings together in groups of three.

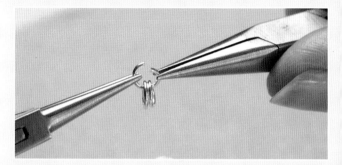

1 Open one jump ring using two pairs of flat- or snipe-nosed pliers, and pick up two more jump rings. Close the jump ring using a reverse action.

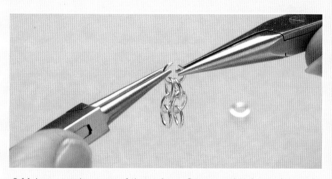

2 Make several groups of three rings. Open another jump ring and add two groups of three rings. Close the ring again.

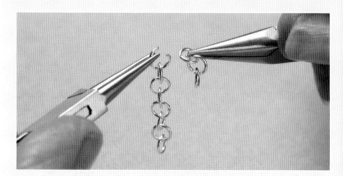

3 Continue adding groups of three with a single jump ring until the chain is as long as you require.

Working with chain

Jewellery chain is available in a variety of styles, materials and quality. Some chains have soldered links to make it much stronger, but many chains are not soldered, so you can open the links with pliers in the same way as jump rings (see opposite) to separate sections if you prefer.

Cutting chain

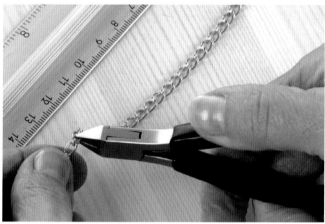

Use the tip of your wire cutters to snip into the links. Measure the length of chain required and then cut through the next link on one side. If the chain is thick or made from hard wire, cut through the other side too so that the link falls away.

Joining chain to fastenings

Use jump rings to attach chain to fastenings or other jewellery findings. Open the jump ring with two pairs of pliers, loop through the last link of the chain, add the fastening and then close the jump ring.

Attaching beads

Bead links or headpin dangles can be added to one or both sides of the chain depending on the style of necklace. Lay the chain down so that it is flat and untwisted, and attach headpin dangles or charms to one side on alternate links, and then if required attach others on the other side to the links in between.

Short lengths of chain are used to join bead links to make this pretty necklace – see Raspberry Rosary, page 65.

Decorative techniques

The majority of necklaces are made using simple stringing techniques, but you can incorporate other beading techniques such as bead stitches and macramé or add pretty findings like sieves and filigree motifs to make more decorative designs.

Tubular herringbone stitch

If you are new to this technique, an easy way to learn it is to work a sample in three different colours. Tubular herringbone stitch is quick to work, as you add two beads at a time. The angle of the beads gives the stitch a wonderful texture, which is enhanced by using triangles or twisted bugles (see Peacock Plume, pages 84–89).

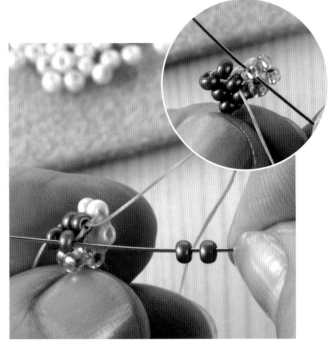

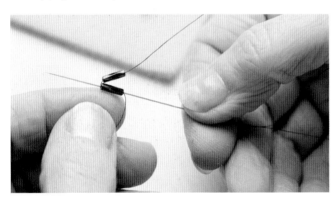

1 To work the ladder stitch base, pick up two bugles (or two seed beads) on a 1.5m (59in) length of beading thread and drop them down near to the end.

2 Pass the needle back through the first bugle and the one just added and pull up taut. Continue adding one bugle (or seed bead) at a time until the ladder stitch band is the length required.

3 To learn herringbone stitch more easily, change colour every two beads. To work, * pick up two beads the same colour as the bead you have just gone through and take the needle back down through the next bead along. Bring the needle back up through the first bead in the next stack. Repeat from * until you reach the first stack again.

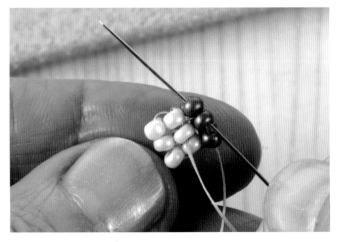

4 To step up ready for the next round, simply take the needle through the top two beads on the next stack. Repeat from * until the rope is the required length.

Macramé

This versatile knotting technique can be used to make a wide range of stunning necklaces. You can begin with the right-hand thread or reverse the knot by starting with the left-hand thread.

Square knot

This simple flat knot is similar to a reef (square) knot (see page 124). Begin by working a half knot over the centre threads.

1 Pass the right-hand thread under the centre threads and over the left-hand thread. Take the left-hand thread across two centre threads and pass it through the loop on the right.

2 Reverse the half knot, passing the left-hand thread under the centre threads and over the right-hand thread. Then take the right-hand thread and pass it through the loop on the left.

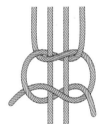

Alternating square knot

This macramé pattern uses two left threads from one knot and two right threads from an adjacent knot to make a knot in the middle.

Adding beads

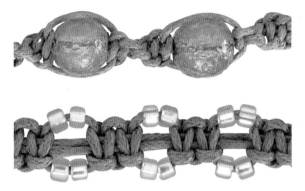

You can add beads to the centre threads, working half knots one after the other, which causes the macramé to spiral round, or add smaller beads on single threads on the outer edge to create a picot effect.

Using a bead sieve

A bead sieve is a piece of mesh, metal or plastic that has holes punched in it so that you can 'sew' beads on to it. Sieves usually form part of a brooch, pendant or other ready-made jewellery items.

You can use the same technique to add beads using thread. Pick up one or two beads on to wire and feed the ends of the wire through two adjacent holes. Feed one wire up through the holes again. Keep adding beads with one wire and then the other until completely covered. Twist the wires at the back to finish.

 Knot know-how

There are several simple knots used in jewellery making that will ensure your necklaces remain intact and fastenings firmly attached. For extra security, add a drop of jewellery glue on the knots and leave to dry before trimming the tails.

Half-hitch

Double half-hitch knot

To secure the tail of your thread, work one or two half-hitches over another thread within the beading. To work, take the needle behind a thread in the beadwork and leave a loop. Pass the needle back through the loop and pull up to make the half-hitch. Repeat for extra security or add a drop of jewellery glue over the knot. Feed the tail through several beads before trimming.

Reef (square)

Reef (square) knot

This is the basic knot for tying two threads of equal thickness. It is fairly secure, but can be loosened by tugging on one end. To tie, pass the left thread over the right and tuck under. Then pass the right thread over the left and tuck under the left thread and out through the gap in the middle.

Overhand

Overhand knot

Use this knot to tie a bundle of threads together or to knot between beads on a string. To tie, simply cross the tail over the main thread to make a small loop, then pass the tail under the thread and back through the loop. You can manoeuvre the knot into position with a tapestry needle (see page 116).

Figure-of-eight

Figure-of-eight knot

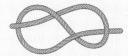

This knot is used to secure a thread in a knot cover (calotte) (see page 114). It makes a fairly large knot that is unlikely to unravel or pull through the hole. To tie, cross the tail in front of the main thread and hold between your finger and thumb so that the loop is facing towards you. Take the tail behind the main thread and pass through the loop from the front. Pull both ends to tighten.

Illusion bead

Illusion bead knot

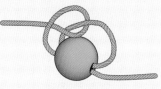

This is a quick knot that can be used to secure large beads on illusion cord (see pages 104–107). To tie, pass the tail through the bead and then go back through, leaving a loose loop. Take the tail through this loop from the underside and then tuck the tail under the new loop. Pull up until taut and add a drop of jewellery glue. Tug the thread out the other side of the bead to hide the knot.

Lark's head

Lark's head knot

This simple knot is used to attach cords and thong to solid rings or to attach threads for macramé. Fold the cord in half and take the loop you have made behind the solid ring so that the loop is visible. Pass the two cord ends through the loop and pull to tighten. To make a reverse lark's head, hold the loop in front of the solid ring and pass the cord ends behind and through the loop.

Bead Details

Bead Details

Bead Shop; gold beads: local bead shop

Lilac Loops, pages 72–73
4mm cubes matte smoky amethyst SB 142FR, seed beads size 6 and 8 dark peach lined crystal AB 275, size ll seed beads matte antique rose F463J: Stitch 'n' Craft

Miracle Bars, page 74
Spacer bars 117465/0349: Kars; faceted beads, miracle beads: Bead Crazy; Delica beads galvanized silver DB35: Stitch 'n' Craft

Captivating Turquoise, page 75
Metal effect beads: local bead shop; miracle beads, ceramic tubes: Bead Crazy; Elements Turquoise spacer beads X1506H-774: Hobbycraft

Lariat, pages 76–83

Twist and Snake, pages 78–81
Double Delica seed beads cinnamon gold lustre DBL 108, lined light blue DBL 58: Stitch 'n' Craft; seed beads size 11 steel blue metallic 460G, light sapphire grey lustre 318B AB and s-l aqua 18, bugles 3mm purple iris metal matte F463: Out On A Whim; glass cylinder beads: The Bead Shop Edinburgh

Flower Fancy, page 82
Seed bead strings size 6 blue-green gloss: Bead Crazy; Lucite flowers and leaves: Bead Time; scarf clips: local bead shop

Rustic Charm, page 83
Beads from a selection: The Bead Shop Edinburgh; resin beads round ribbed ivory 117465/4532: Kars

Chain Reaction, page 83
Beads from a selection: Bead Crazy

Sautoir, pages 84–91

Peacock Plume, pages 86–89
Twisted bugles 773840 9365: Gütermann; seed beads size 11 sapphire purple lustre AB 319K, short bugles 3mm nickel matte F451D, seed beads size 6 nickel matte F451D: Out On A Whim; Toho triangles size 11 blue iris metallic matte 82F: Out On A Whim; glazed ceramic bead, metal filigree beads grey: local bead shop

Linked in Time, page 90
Antique gold beads round ribbed 117465/2634, round hammered 117465/2648, oval 117467/2652, square flat 117465/2638: Kars; glazed ceramic beads 15mm cream: Bead Crazy; cut glass crystal brown 25 x 35mm: The Bead Shop Edinburgh

Midnight and Moonshine, page 91
Black agate 14mm string, black agate 10mm string, black onyx frosted 6mm string, black onyx frosted 4mm string: Ilona Biggins; antique silver beads: Bead Crazy

Lime and Raspberry Splash, page 91
Faceted bead fuchsia 24 x 36mm 15 032 276, faceted bead fuchsia 18mm 15 034 276, pearl round purple velvet 16mm 14 332 318, pearl round jade four 16mm 14 332 432, pearl-shaped 22 x 26mm jade 14 331 432, purple velvet 14 331 318: Rayher Hobby; seed beads size 11 transparent lime, glass pearl 10 mm jade and purple: Bead Crazy; topaz raspberry lustre AB318L: Out On A Whim

Knotted Necklace, pages 92–101

Macramé Magic, pages 94–97
Pony beads, large donut green: Hobbycraft; yarn: Ingrid de Vane

Textural Key Charm, page 97
Cube bead, yarn: Ingrid de Vane

Fruity Fun, pages 98–99
Beads from a selection: Bead Crazy

Wood Works, page 100
Craft Factory Natural World dark wood beads CF05/48A (42mm), 48B (50mm), 101 (round): Gütermann; painted wood and coloured beads: Bead Crazy

Candy Cords, page 101
Beads from a selection: Bead Crazy; crocheted beads antique rose 15 00036: Rayher Hobby

Floating Necklace, pages 102–111

Silver Sensation, pages 104–107
Beads from a selection: The Bead Shop Edinburgh

Funky Lime, pages 108–109
Mixed plastic beads, miracle beads: Bead Crazy

Crystal Falls, page 110
Beads from a selection: The Bead Shop Edinburgh

Pearl Illusion, page 111
Shaped turquoise beads: Bead Crazy; pearls, round metal-effect beads, pressed glass green mottled: Viking Loom

Suppliers and Acknowledgments

Suppliers

UK & Europe

Bead Crazy
55 George Street
Perth PH1 5LB
Tel: 01738 442288
Email: info@beadcrazy.co.uk
www.beadcrazy.co.uk

Bead Time
5 Church Road
Ashford
Middlesex T15 2UG
Tel: 01784 252438
www.beadtime.co.uk

Beads and Bling
5 Bedford Row
Temple Bar
Dublin 2
Tel: (01) 6337814
www.beadsandbling.com

Craftime
Unit B2 Site 3 Willow Drive
Sherwood Business Park
Annesley
Nottingham NG15 0DP
Tel: 01623 722828
Email: sales@craftime.co.uk
www.craftime.co.uk

Ingrid de Vane
Mill House
Sandford Orcas
Sherbourne
Dorset DT9 4SB
Tel: 01963 220231
Email: idevane@aol.com
www.ingrid-de-vane.co.uk

Gütermann
Perivale-Gütermann Ltd
Bullsbrook Road
Hayes
Middlesex UB4 0JR
Tel: 0208 589 1600
Email: perivale@guetermann.com

Hobbycraft
Tel: 0800 027 2387 for nearest store
Mail order tel: 01202 596100

Ilona Biggins
PO Box 600
Rickmansworth
WD3 5WR
Tel: 01923 282998
Email: info@ilonabiggins.co.uk
www.ilonabiggins.co.uk

Kars
UK Office
PO Box 272
Aylesbury
Buckinghamshire HP18 9FH
Tel: 01844 238080
Email: info@kars.nl
www.kars.biz

Rayher Hobby
Fockestrasse 15
88471 Laupeim
Germany
Tel: 07392 7005 0
Email: info@rayher-hobby.de
www.rayher-hobby.de

Stitch 'n' Craft
Swans Yard Craft Centre
High Street
Shaftesbury
Dorset SP7 8JQ
Mail order tel: 01747 830666
Email: enquiries@stitchncraft.co.uk
www.stitchncraft.co.uk

The Bead Shop Edinburgh
6 Dean Park Street
Stockbridge
Edinburgh EH4 1JW
Tel: 0131 343 3222
Email: info@beadshopedinburgh.co.uk
www.beadshopscotland.co.uk

The Little Bead Shop
96 Bruntsfield Place
Edinburgh
EH10 9NX
Tel: 0131 228 5058
www.thelittlebeadshop.co.uk

The Mineral Warehouse
Tel: 01903 877037
Email: sales@minware.co.uk
www.minware.co.uk

USA

Firemountain Gems and Beads
1 Fire Mountain Way
Grants Pass OR 97526-2373
Tel: 1-541-956-7890
www.firemountaingems.com

Harlequin Beads
1027 Willamette Street
Eugene OR 97401
Tel: 1-541-683-5903
Email: info@harlequinbead.com
www.harlequinbead.com

Jewellery Supply
301 Derek Place
Roseville CA 95678
Tel: 1-916-780-610
Email: help@jewellerysupply.com
www.jewellerysupply.com

Land of Odds
718 Thomson Lane
Ste 123
Nashville TN 37204
Tel: 1-615-292-0610
Email: oddsian@landofodds.com
www.landofodds.com

Out On A Whim
121 E Cotati Ave
Cotati CA 94931
Tel: 1-707-664-8343
www.whimbeads.com

Acknowledgments

I have thoroughly enjoyed creating the projects for this book, and as I recently moved back to Scotland, it has given me a great opportunity to search out some of the super bead shops here. I would especially like to thank Maxine Griffiths, the proprietor of Bead Crazy, for her support and encouragement. I would also like to thank all the other suppliers who provided beads and materials: Craftime, Gütermann, Hobbycraft, Kars and Rayher Hobby. Contact details are given above.

About the Author and Index

About the Author

Dorothy Wood is an expert beader, crafter and author who has written over 20 craft books on a variety of subjects. This is her seventh beading book for David and Charles, her previous book being the bestselling *The Beader's Bible*. She also contributes to several well-known craft magazines, including *Beautiful Cards* and *Knit Today*. Dorothy lives in Upper Largo, Fife, Scotland, and can be contacted via her website, www.dorothywood.co.uk.

Index